The *Authentic* STANDARDS-BASED ENVIRONMENT

A SYSTEMATIC APPROACH TO LEARNING TARGETS, ASSESSMENT, AND DATA

EILEEN DEPKA

Solution Tree | Press

a division of
Solution Tree

555 North Morton Street
Bloomington, IN 47404
800.733.6786 (toll free) / 812.336.7700
FAX: 812.336.7790

email: info@SolutionTree.com
SolutionTree.com

Visit **go.SolutionTree.com/assessment** to download the free reproducibles in this book.

Printed in the United States of America

Library of Congress Cataloging-in-Publication Data

Names: Depka, Eileen, author.
Title: The authentic standards-based environment : a systematic approach to
   learning targets, assessment, and data / Eileen Depka.
Description: Bloomington, IN : Solution Tree Press, 2022. | Includes
   bibliographical references and index.
Identifiers: LCCN 2022010775 (print) | LCCN 2022010776 (ebook) | ISBN
   9781954631250 (paperback) | ISBN 9781954631267 (ebook)
Subjects: LCSH: Education--Standards--United States. | Effective
   teaching--United States. | Academic achievement--United States--Testing.
   | Educational tests and measurements--United States.
Classification: LCC LB3060.83 .D47 2022 (print) | LCC LB3060.83 (ebook) |
   DDC 379.1/580973--dc23/eng/20220617
LC record available at https://lccn.loc.gov/2022010775
LC ebook record available at https://lccn.loc.gov/2022010776

Solution Tree
Jeffrey C. Jones, CEO
Edmund M. Ackerman, President

Solution Tree Press
President and Publisher: Douglas M. Rife
Associate Publisher: Sarah Payne-Mills
Managing Production Editor: Kendra Slayton
Editorial Director: Todd Brakke
Art Director: Rian Anderson
Copy Chief: Jessi Finn
Production Editor: Miranda Addonizio
Content Development Specialist: Amy Rubenstein
Acquisitions Editor: Sarah Jubar
Copy Editor: Jessi Finn
Proofreader: Elisabeth Abrams
Text Designer: Fabiana Cochran
Associate Editor: Sarah Ludwig
Editorial Assistants: Charlotte Jones and Elijah Oates

ACKNOWLEDGMENTS

Special thanks to Miranda Addonizio, editor extraordinaire. With persistence and patience, she guided me through the editing process.

Thank you to the truly phenomenal staff at Solution Tree, who promote all that is best in education by providing high-quality materials. Special accolades to Douglas Rife and Sarah Payne-Mills and all who made this book a possibility.

Thanks to the educators who provided feedback and embraced the processes within this book.

Solution Tree Press would like to thank the following reviewers:

Chris Bennett
    Principal
    Burns Middle School
    Lawndale, North Carolina

Mandi Dunlap
    Principal
    Greenbrier Eastside Elementary
    Greenbrier, Arkansas

Nicholas A. Emmanuele
    English Teacher and Department Chair
    McDowell Intermediate High School
    Erie, Pennsylvania

John D. Ewald
    Education Consultant
    Frederick, Maryland

Jenna Fanshier
    Sixth-Grade Teacher
    Hesston Middle School
    Hesston, Kansas

Doug Gee
    Superintendent
    Clear Lake Community School District
    Clear Lake, Iowa

Visit **go.SolutionTree.com/assessment** to download the free reproducibles in this book.

TABLE OF CONTENTS

Reproducible pages are in italics.

ABOUT THE AUTHOR

Eileen Depka, PhD, has a background in assessment, common assessment design, rubric development, standards-based assessment, question design, classroom questioning practices, positive practices in grading and reporting, and implementation of standards-based grading and reporting. She is the author and coauthor of many books, including *Bringing Homework Into Focus, Using Formative Assessment in the RTI Framework, Designing Rubrics for Mathematics, Designing Assessment for Mathematics,* and *The Data Guidebook for Teachers and Leaders.*

Eileen has supervised and coordinated curriculum, instruction, assessment, special education, educational technology, and continuous improvement efforts. She has taught all subjects at the elementary and middle school levels as well as graduate-level courses. She provides professional development for K–12 and undergraduate educators and, as a consultant, has worked across the United States, focusing on creating engaging workshops tailored to meet a school's and district's individual needs. She is passionate about student achievement and believes that all students can find academic success. Her goal is to work with teachers and administrators to collectively increase expertise and add to strategy banks used in schools to increase student performance.

Eileen earned a bachelor's degree in elementary- and middle-level education from the University of Wisconsin–Milwaukee, and she earned her master's and doctoral degrees from Cardinal Stritch University.

To learn more about Eileen's work, follow @eileen_depka on Twitter.

To book Eileen Depka for professional development, contact pd@SolutionTree.com.

INTRODUCTION

Having been a classroom teacher for a number of years, I used to find myself questioning why my fellow teachers and I had to engage in certain initiatives. For example, some initiatives asked that we learn difficult-to-understand and seemingly meaningless vocabulary for programs that had no effect on student progress. They asked that we post in the classroom the numbers of standards we used without helping us realize the standards' importance or the fact that we needed to communicate the standards to the students. They asked that we break down standards without understanding how to utilize the information. They asked that we create learning targets without giving us a basis in what information to use or how to effectively share the targets with students. Sometimes, I just didn't understand how the pieces fit into the big picture of student learning. I wondered whether the work on which we focused would make a difference. When I became engaged in working with standards in a more deliberate and intentional way, those questions disappeared. I saw the connections. I understood the alignment. If you have had those same questions, my hope is that, after reading this book, you will see the crucial nature of standards and the same usefulness that I do.

The sole purpose of this book is to provide direction that supports a systematic approach to standards-based student learning. It is intended for individuals, schools, or districts as a training and implementation tool. It is a resource for all who desire to implement a logical, comprehensive approach to take student learning all the way from standards to a response to assessment data.

This book gives down-to-earth, step-by-step guidance for creating a truly standards-based environment. It provides sensible information that teachers can implement without difficulty. Each chapter follows the same approach, leading to a complete look at student learning. This approach inspires insights into standards, assessment, and data that result in enhanced classroom possibilities. Let's take a look at the significance of learning standards; then we'll go over the content and organization of this book.

SUPPORT OF STANDARDS

Why implement standards? First, let's discuss what exactly standards are and what problems they are designed to address. *Standards* are written descriptions that provide a common focus regarding what students should know and be able to do by the end of a period of time. Having a road map of what students are to achieve gives us educators guidance throughout the year. Standards even allow us to see previous and future expectations; they give us a target to aim for when developing everything from assessments to lessons to remediation, acceleration, and beyond.

The implementation of a coordinated standards-based system is important to student success. According to Robert J. Marzano, an education author, researcher, and leader, "Standards hold the greatest hope for significantly improving student achievement" (as cited in Scherer, 2001, p. 14). Robert J. Marzano and Professional Learning Communities at Work® architect Robert Eaker assert schools that effectively implement a standards-based or competency-based system:

> create students who move through the curriculum at a pace that is consistent with their development and individual needs. Additionally, students are less likely to have gaps in their learning and are more likely to develop an enhanced sense of agency and responsibility. (Eaker & Marzano, 2020, p. 14)

The clear guidance that standards provide about what students should learn and be able to do by the end of each grade level and course is a springboard for many educational possibilities. The use of standards supports rigor in the classroom (Herk, 2015). Standards serve to ensure transparency in all aspects of teaching and learning while identifying that which is considered most important to teach (Guskey, 2016). Classrooms each deliberately focus on the same aspects of student learning when their teachers implement standards, providing consistency among classrooms and across schools, districts, states, and provinces.

Breaking down standards into student learning targets creates clarity for teachers and students because doing so ensures teachers can easily identify learning expectations. Assessments tied to both standards and targets help teachers measure how well students can demonstrate these expectations.

The process of using standards and developing standards-based assessments ensures that all students in a school, district, state or province, or country are on a level playing field with common learning expectations. Assessments directly related to the standards serve to measure students' achievement of what they need to know and be able to do during the current school year, and these assessments act as building blocks for the future. Standards-based assessments give educators an understanding of how student learning is progressing for individuals and groups (Center on Standards and Assessment Implementation, 2018). Teachers can track assessment results across years, creating a picture of student growth over time.

Teachers do not find themselves needing to determine what they will teach in isolation from others at their grade level. The skills and concepts necessary for students to succeed are identified for not only the current school year but also the grade levels that follow. When we teachers rely on standards, the path to teaching and learning is clear and consistent. We know that colleagues are teaching the same standards, which promotes our ability to collaborate and realize a shared focus (Schmoker & Marzano, 1999). Standards improve the probability that achievement and equity will increase because they provide a framework that allows teachers to align academic content with other teachers. This ensures consistency of learning expectations across classrooms, districts, and states or provinces (Kornhaber, Barkauskas, & Griffith, 2016). Standards take the guesswork out of *what* to teach, yet they allow great freedom in *how* to teach it. Teachers have an identified target, but how they reach that target depends on students' needs, available resources, and their own creativity. The benefits of standards-based learning extend to parents as well. Parents can gain assurance that their children will be held to the same standards as others.

The logical applicability of standards is not limited to K–12 schools. Consider what could happen, for example, if those studying to be pilots didn't have consistent standards. What if the knowledge and skills pilots learned were totally dependent on individual instructors? While the individual instructors might have the best intentions, they wouldn't necessarily know what others in their field have determined as the key concepts. A more reliable system of common standards is the safer and more reasonable approach to education in K–12 classrooms and beyond. The objective is for students to have the same potential for and possibility of success no matter where they live or receive their education.

Classroom teachers, teacher teams, districts, or states or provinces can select resources that align with the standards. Whoever selects the resources, the standards give them direction as to what to look for. Resources can include everything from texts to assessments to supplementary materials for programs valuable to implementing the standards. When stakeholders obtain standards-aligned materials, they know they won't be wasting their money on resources that won't improve student learning. That is because the resources contain the necessary content from the standards; this alignment guarantees the materials will support implementation of the standards at each grade level. The use of standards-aligned materials will support teachers' knowledge, reinforcing their ability to help students master the standards (Kaufman, Opfer, Bongard, Pane, & Thompson, 2018).

Advocating for the implementation of standards makes sense. Identifying high standards and then using them to create a systematic approach to student learning will result in a more coherent and more effective educational system (McCluskey, 2010).

THE CONTENT

The pages that follow include a step-by-step look at evaluating standards and using that information to plan for and design learning targets, classroom assessments, rubrics, common assessments, data formats, and scope-and-sequence possibilities. The final chapter features a planning guide to assist you in applying this book's contents on a journey to implement standards-based learning across classrooms, schoolwide, or even districtwide.

This book uses a simple approach that connects different aspects of learning, resulting in a system that is easy to implement. The connections make it easy to see how one task fits with the next. Standards provide direction and focus, which take the guesswork out of determining what students should know and be able to do. Teachers should use standards not in isolation but as an integral part of a systematic approach to teaching and learning. Figure I.1 illustrates how standards fit into the bigger picture and the key areas this book highlights. All aspects of learning flow from and constantly circle the standards. The tasks circling the standards are cyclical, each one following another to create a system of standards-based implementation that is doable and sensible. This process interlocks with my system of assessment I presented in *Letting Data Lead* (Depka, 2019). In this book, we will focus on the pieces that make this system possible: standards, learning targets, assessments, rubrics, and data.

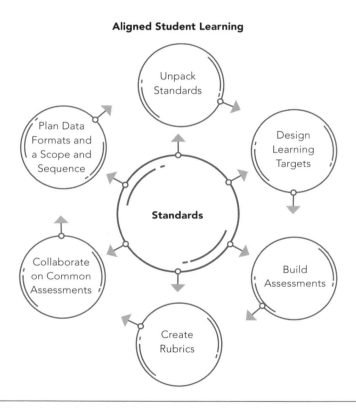

FIGURE I.1: How aligned student learning flows from the standards.

The beauty of this systemic approach is in its simplicity. The power of the system lies in how each component connects to the next, supplying valuable information to teachers and students. This book explains each component as it progresses from task to task and chapter to chapter.

AN OVERVIEW

This book uses the Common Core State Standards (National Governors Association Center for Best Practices [NGA] & Council of Chief State School Officers [CCSSO], 2010a, 2010b) for most examples because these well-known standards serve as a useful baseline. However, to show how broadly useful this standards-based approach to assessment and beyond is, I have also brought in examples from the standards of Texas and British Columbia. Whatever standards your school or district uses, this system will work.

The examples throughout the book mostly concentrate on kindergarten through grade 5 and feature English language arts and mathematics standards. However, these methods are easily applicable to all grade levels, including secondary grades, and all content areas. Secondary examples appear in chapters 1 and 2 to help establish this applicability and illustrate that teachers at the secondary level can use the processes throughout the remaining chapters. From chapter 3 on, I focus on examples at the elementary level, as I am not a content expert in the secondary grades. But I have worked with many secondary teachers who have been very successful in following these examples and recommendations.

I have divided this book into the following three parts and seven chapters; all procedures in the chapters are illustrated with multiple examples.

Part 1 concerns laying the foundation for a standards-based system.

- **Chapter 1:** This chapter provides the basis for all that follows by explaining how to unpack standards, which underlies each task in the remaining chapters. Basically, to *unpack* a standard means to take the standard apart in a logical way to best understand the components and expectations it comprises. This approach allows teachers to clearly and simply explain the standard to students, giving them a true understanding of the expected learning outcomes.

- **Chapter 2:** This chapter explains how to use an unpacked standard to design standards-based learning targets that directly relate to each component of the standard. The learning targets let students know what the standard expects by showing them the steps necessary to successfully demonstrate their knowledge. The direct connection between the standard and the learning targets makes the targets meaningful and useful for students; targets are precise and specific so that students can easily relate them to what it takes to master the standard. That way, students understand exactly what they need to know and be able to do in order to succeed.

Part 2 covers the tools and analysis—assessments, rubrics, and data reporting—that teachers must master to create a standards-based environment in which they and students can truly thrive.

- **Chapter 3:** This chapter is all about assessment design. Each design starts with the unpacked standard, which guides assessment development and determines the rigor associated with the standard. Two tools are especially valuable when determining rigor: (1) Lorin W. Anderson and David R. Krathwohl's (2001) update to Benjamin Bloom's (1954) taxonomy and (2) Norman Webb's (2002) Depth of Knowledge (Francis, 2022). Several examples show the direct connection between the standard and the assessment. The chapter also contains a variety of assessment formats. Whether you are creating your own or identifying an existing assessment, this chapter gives guidance to ensure the assessment is standards based.

- **Chapter 4:** This chapter illustrates the development of standards-based rubrics, again starting with the unpacked standard. The rubrics bring standards to life. They provide a road map that increases the potential for student success. The chapter includes several examples to evaluate the processes associated with various standards.

- **Chapter 5:** This chapter concentrates on common assessments and their benefits. It exemplifies how to build a standards-based common assessment, starting as usual with the unpacked standard, and embeds several teacher-team discussion questions. These questions are designed to inspire discussions that will help teams implement common assessments in a truly common way. The goal is to set the stage for teacher discussions based on comparable data. A variety of common assessment examples are included throughout the chapter. Rubrics developed in chapter 4 can also be used as the basis for common assessment, scoring, and teacher discussion.

- **Chapter 6:** This chapter uses unpacked standards (and the assessments designed to test them) for two purposes. First, it identifies formats for reporting data. The method the chapter illustrates ties data directly to how students are performing on each component of the standard, allowing teachers to have a clear picture of students' strengths and their challenge areas. The standards-based data reports help teachers identify obvious next steps when reteaching because each part of the report directly relates to the components of the standard.

  Second, the chapter examines an unpacked document containing all standards for an entire category under a content area. This document, in its entirety, allows readers to understand the scope and depth of the learning required to adequately perform in this area. Readers can use the document for planning, identifying resources, and developing a more global scope and sequence.

Part 3 broadens the scope to discuss implementation of a standards-based environment at the school or district level.

- **Chapter 7:** This chapter serves a different purpose than the other chapters do. It is intended to provide suggestions and support for teachers, schools, and districts so they can implement the practices highlighted in this book on a wider scale. It shares tips for establishing a common sense of purpose and creating a sense of urgency. It also includes a method to track progress, as well as team discussion questions to promote both collaboration and continued progress.

Collectively, the chapters will provide a connected process for implementing a standards-based approach to teaching and learning. This implementation process is systematic, informative, and logical. Multiple examples throughout highlight the connectedness of the implementation, giving credence to the essential nature of standards. No matter what standards are the basis for your curriculum, this approach will work for you.

Does any of this sound intimidating? Please don't let it. I promise that I effectively support the explanations and processes with examples that illuminate the method. Step-by-step instructions will help get you well on your way to understanding standards-based processes and developing your own resources. I believe you will see that this approach makes sense for you and your students. I have confidence that you will be successful in your efforts to implement the ideas this book contains.

PART 1

THE FOUNDATION

LEARNING TARGETS

STANDARDS

UNDERSTANDING

Chapter 1 lays the foundation for the process the rest of the book describes. Chapter 2 provides a foundation for students to make sense of their learning and make direct connections to the standards.

UNPACKING STANDARDS: WHY AND HOW

When I started teaching, I knew what to teach. I did exactly what the text and resources I was given told me to do. Though I felt like I knew what I was doing, I was clueless. Then I started talking with the teachers in the grades above and below me. We had a great team. Everyone was doing their best. Everyone was using their resources. We discovered that in some cases, our resources were different, with eye-opening overlaps and gaps. Even the resources that were consistent gave us some cause for concern. Who should teach what? How would we fill the gaps? Standards were the answer. This discovery might seem obvious, but for us, it was a revelation. Standards could lead the way, help us with alignment, and guarantee that we focused on what our students truly needed to know and do. This was a new beginning on a path important to student success.

Standards provide the foundation for all that is to come with teaching and learning. They are the guiding authority, and they are the key to consistency and connections to every part of the learning process. They support a vision that is followed by expectations and details of all aspects of student learning. Standards are rich in information, but they can be hard to parse. To understand them, we teachers need to find an efficient and useful way to analyze them. Unpacking a standard allows us to interpret its meaning (Wiggins & McTighe, 2012).

In this chapter, we'll discuss the importance of the unpacking process, how to engage in this process, and the importance of sharing unpacked standards with students.

WHY UNPACKING THE STANDARDS IS ESSENTIAL

Understanding the standards is the first step to understanding every aspect of classroom learning. They present the foundation that takes us from teaching and assessment to student success. The vision that standards provide becomes clear as we look more deeply into them. Think of the joys of uncovering the layers of a fascinating piece of literature in a close reading. By breaking down and delving into what the piece incorporates, we come to a clear and purposeful understanding. Standards provide that same clarity of purpose when we look at how the building blocks fit together. So how do we gain this depth of knowledge? We disaggregate. We deconstruct. For the purposes of this book, we will call it *unpacking* the standards. Whatever we call it, the result leads to an exceptional understanding of what the standard is asking of us. The process of unpacking reveals the specific learning expectations as well as the level of rigor required.

Whether we call it *disaggregating, unwrapping,* or *unpacking,* the purpose remains the same: to provide clarity and understanding of standards to teachers and students alike. I find unpacking an enlightening process, as the depth that this practice exposes with some standards is remarkable. When I first became acquainted with the term *unpacking,* I had my doubts. Was it a fad? Was it just another initiative that would waste everyone's time and soon be gone? The answer to both questions is *absolutely not!* The clarity gained through unpacking is an incredible start to making sense of standards, and linking the unpacked standards to all aspects of teaching and learning provides such a systematic approach that it just makes sense. The step-by-step approach revealed in the English language arts standards for writing, for example, provides a road map to successful writing.

When I realized the impact the unpacking process can have on student learning, I was sold. As I developed the process that I describe in this book, I began to truly understand the intricacies of the standards and how to use them. The added clarity was also important in helping me transfer that information to increase student understanding. Clarity is crucial for teachers, and the impact that deeper understanding can have on students is essential. Achievement is much more likely to improve when students understand the what and why of all that their teachers expect them to learn (Farnsworth, 2017). My goal is to make the unpacking process simple, sensible, doable, and connected.

This chapter introduces a method for unpacking standards that has a number of specific benefits worth mentioning.

- The goal of unpacking a standard is to create a document that states each component of the standard. I call this an *unpacked standards document* or just an *unpacked document.* Creating this document promotes a better understanding of the standard and the expectations it contains.

- The unpacked document is a road map to successful achievement. Present this document to students as a visual display. For example, if we unpack the English language arts standard, "Write opinion pieces on topics or texts, supporting a point of view with reasons and information" (W.4.1; NGA & CCSSO, 2010a), we can let students know they will be writing an opinion piece, and we can share with them every component of that standard as listed in the unpacked document.

- The unpacked document provides us with guidance on the order in which we might teach lessons. For example, with W.4.1 (NGA & CCSSO, 2010a), we might first teach students how to write an appropriate introduction. We can use each row of the document chart to formulate lessons and provide students with instructions necessary to be successful. When lessons are complete, students will be able to show their expertise on the entire standard.

- We can share the document with students when they're writing their opinion pieces to remind them of all essential components of the standard. This reminder will help students complete higher-quality pieces because the task is clear and delineated.

- We can use each row of the unpacked document to develop a learning target or outcome that we share with students. I will illustrate this in chapter 2 (page 31).

- We can use the unpacked document to develop assessments at appropriate levels of rigor and completeness. I will explore this in chapter 3 (page 47).

- The unpacked document becomes the basis for a rubric. This will be the subject of chapter 4 (page 67).

Teachers who unpack standards gain a deep understanding of the components within. Aligning standards and assessments allows teachers to focus on identifying and quickly reacting to student needs. The unpacked standards give teachers a sense of confidence that they truly understand what students need to know and be able to do in order to experience success (Nielsen, 2016). Furthermore, unpacking standards works to distinguish minor and major aspects of the standards, providing insights into how to sequence learning. Understanding individual components of the standards assists teachers in identifying specific student learning strengths and challenges; and when teachers know with such specificity what support students need, they can more effectively provide it (Schimmer, 2016b).

When it comes to unpacking standards, there may be concern that teachers will focus too much on teaching discrete skills, sacrificing higher-order thinking and conceptual understanding by not connecting these skills back to the whole standard (Kansas State Department of Education, 2011). The standards-based process in this book is designed to make teachers very conscious of the depth and contents of the standards; this way, teachers can guide students in learning the basics while linking these pieces of what they need to know and be able to do to the bigger picture. Consider all that goes into having students write a nonfiction report for the first time, for example. They need to know how to do research, how to write coherent sentences, how to combine sentences into a logical paragraph, how to get the information across clearly throughout the whole report, how to add illustrations to support their points, and much more. When we teachers break this process into pieces, we might start with writing a good introduction. But we don't stop there. Once the students understand the first piece, we build on that by including the next step, then the next, until they have learned all the components, they understand how the components contribute to the whole, and they can use the components to demonstrate understanding of the entire process of writing a report. Imagine bypassing all of that and just asking students to write a report. In the same way, breaking down the standard helps students understand exactly what they need to know and do to succeed with the whole. Without unpacking the standard into its logical components, the whole can be overwhelming and confusing. Start with the pieces, and build to a successful performance of the entire standard.

HOW THE PROCESS WORKS: UNPACKING, DECONSTRUCTING, OR DISAGGREGATING

All three words—(1) *unpacking*, (2) *deconstructing*, and (3) *disaggregating*—mean the same thing. Choose one to use, and know that no matter what we call it, the depth of understanding we, as educators, gain through the process stays the same. The expectations of standards become clear to teachers and students alike. Unpacked standards are crucial and are clearly the primary source of learning expectations.

So, what is the process? Once you have chosen a standard to unpack, charting its key components and creating an unpacked document comprise three steps.

1. Find all verbs and actions stated within the standard.

2. Locate the components of the standard that receive the actions.

3. Determine whether there is any additional information worth including.

You place the information in a chart like that pictured in figure 1.1. You list the standard, then unpack it. I will expand on this chart, which I call the *unpacked standards document*, in the following chapters to display and organize additional information, including learning targets. A full-page reproducible version is available on page 29.

Content Area:		
Specific Standard:		
Verbs or Actions	**Receivers of the Actions**	**Additional Information** (What, where, why, how, examples, teacher notes)

FIGURE 1.1: Template for an unpacked standards document.

To illustrate the method, we'll start with Common Core Reading—Literature standard 4 for grade 5, which states, "Determine the meaning of words and phrases as they are used in a text, including figurative language such as metaphors and similes" (RL.5.4; NGA & CCSSO, 2010a).

To begin breaking down the standard, highlight verbs and actions, and underline what receives the actions. Then follow the three steps as they appear in figures 1.2, 1.3, and 1.4.

1. Note the highlighted verbs and actions in the standard. Place these in the first column of the chart. In this case, the verbs are *determine* and *include* (figure 1.2).

2. Identify the underlined receivers of the actions. What are the students being asked to determine and include? We can see that the standard asks the students to determine the meaning of words and include figurative language. Place those words (*meaning of words* and *figurative language*) in the Receivers of the Actions column (figure 1.3).

3. Decide whether any additional information is needed to better understand the standard. Often, none is. The object here is not to list every word in the standard but to use what is essential. We can use the words *in a text* to best understand where students are to find the words and phrases. This may be obvious to teachers, but since we want to use the unpacked documents with students as well, we include it rather than taking it for granted (figure 1.4).

Content Area: English Language Arts (Reading—Literature)		
Specific Standard: RL.5.4—**Determine** the meaning of words and phrases as they are used in a text, **including figurative language** such as metaphors and similes.		
Verbs or Actions	**Receivers of the Actions**	**Additional Information**
Determine		
Include		

Source for standard: NGA & CCSSO, 2010a.

FIGURE 1.2: Example unpacked standard for Reading—Literature standard 4, grade 5, step 1.

Content Area: English Language Arts (Reading—Literature)		
Specific Standard: RL.5.4—**Determine** the meaning of words and phrases as they are used in a text, **including figurative language** such as metaphors and similes.		
Verbs or Actions	**Receivers of the Actions**	**Additional Information**
Determine	Meaning of words	
Include	Figurative language	

Source for standard: NGA & CCSSO, 2010a.

FIGURE 1.3: Example unpacked standard for Reading—Literature standard 4, grade 5, step 2.

Content Area: English Language Arts (Reading—Literature)		
Specific Standard: RL.5.4—**Determine** the meaning of words and phrases as they are used in a text, **including figurative language** such as metaphors and similes.		
Verbs or Actions	**Receivers of the Actions**	**Additional Information**
Determine	Meaning of words	In a text
Include	Figurative language	

Source for standard: NGA & CCSSO, 2010a.

FIGURE 1.4: Example unpacked standard for Reading—Literature standard 4, grade 5, step 3.

Notice that figure 1.4 (page 13) provides an easy-to-interpret view of the entire standard, breaking it down into smaller parts. The broken-down standard parts will be used throughout the next chapters to build learning targets, assessments, rubrics, and more.

In this and future chapters, I often unpack one standard at a time for the sake of exemplification. Unpacking one at a time allows us to see at a glance how to unpack complex standards and how to pay attention to important words like *and* and *or*. I recommend, however, when unpacking in earnest, that you create unpacked documents by strand, domain, or whatever grouping of standards the document uses within a content area—and I have included some examples of those documents as well. As you begin to unpack standards, it will become clear which standards are more complex than others. Teachers often consider these more complex standards to be learning priorities and may give them additional consideration during the teaching process.

UNPACKING ONE STANDARD AT A TIME

Some standards provide an overarching summary prior to listing each individual component. The Common Core Writing standards are good examples. Review the fourth-grade standard for writing in figure 1.5.

Content Area: English Language Arts (Writing)

Specific Standard: W.4.1—Write opinion pieces on topics or texts, supporting a point of view with reasons and information.
- a. Introduce a topic or text clearly, state an opinion, and create an organizational structure in which related ideas are grouped to support the writer's purpose.
- b. Provide reasons that are supported by facts and details.
- c. Link opinion and reasons using words and phrases (e.g., *for instance, in order to, in addition*).
- d. Provide a concluding statement or section related to the opinion presented.

Verbs or Actions	Receivers of the Actions	Additional Information (What, where, why, how, examples, teacher notes)
Introduce	Topic or text	
State	Opinion	
Create	Organizational structure	To group ideas To support the author's purpose
Provide	Reasons	
Support	Reasons	With facts and details
Link	Opinions and Reasons	
Link using	Words and Phrases	Examples: *for instance, in order to, in addition*
Provide	Concluding statement or section	Related to the opinion

Source for standard: NGA & CCSSO, 2010a.

FIGURE 1.5: Example unpacked document for Writing standard 1, grade 4.

The standard states the task that students are to complete. Then, the points that follow (a, b, c, and d) each dictate the individual components required to adequately perform the task. The teacher should unpack the components to illustrate the detailed skills the students are expected to perform, providing extreme clarity. In fact, including the overarching task is optional because it tells students what they are going to do, while the individual components tell them how they are actually expected to complete the task.

Notice as in the previous examples, the Verbs or Actions column contains the verbs or actions from the standard, the Receivers of the Actions column states what receives the actions, and the Additional Information column contains any additional information. This process is consistent, and we will use it every time we unpack standards.

The standard in figure 1.5 has two words worth mentioning: (1) *and* and (2) *or*. When a standard uses the word *or*, it indicates choice. When it uses *and*, students need to demonstrate both for mastery. This standard states that students can write opinions on topics *or* texts. Teachers can leave the choice up to students or select one themselves. The standard also mentions that students are to use facts *and* details. In this case, there is no element of choice because the standard indicates they are to do both.

Figure 1.6 provides an alternative example of how we might unpack W.4.1. Note that some actions shift from the third column to the first column. Those changes are indicated with an asterisk.

Content Area: English Language Arts (Writing)		

Specific Standard: W.4.1—Write opinion pieces on topics or texts, supporting a point of view with reasons and information.
   a. Introduce a topic or text clearly, state an opinion, and create an organizational structure in which related ideas are grouped to support the writer's purpose.
   b. Provide reasons that are supported by facts and details.
   c. Link opinion and reasons using words and phrases (e.g., *for instance, in order to, in addition*).
   d. Provide a concluding statement or section related to the opinion presented.		

Verbs or Actions	**Receivers of the Actions**	**Additional Information** (What, where, why, how, examples, teacher notes)
Introduce	Topic or text	
State	Opinion	
Create	Organizational structure	
*Group	Ideas	
*Support	Author's purpose	
Provide	Reasons	
*Provide	Facts and Details	
Link	Opinions and Reasons	
Link using	Words and Phrases	Examples: *for instance, in order to, in addition*
Provide	Concluding statement or section	Related to the opinion

Source for standard: NGA & CCSSO, 2010a.

FIGURE 1.6: Alternative unpacked document for Writing standard 1, grade 4.

Moving these portions of the standard emphasizes their importance, but it no longer clearly links them to the part of the standard that immediately precedes them. For example, standard

W.4.1 says that students should provide facts and details for the reasons they state, which is how figure 1.5 (page 14) lists it. In figure 1.6 (page 15), providing facts and details is listed separately, which adds emphasis to both listing reasons and providing facts and details. Either format will work depending on how we interpret the standard. Both will support students in meeting the standard. Feel free to be flexible, and list the actions in the way that will best illustrate the components of the standards for your students. Share the unpacked document with the students so they can see each component that is expected of them when writing an opinion. The list will provide a clear and visual reminder of exactly what students need to accomplish in order to meet the standard.

Before moving on, let's take a look at an unpacked Common Core Writing standard at the secondary level. This example creates an outline of what students are to include in their writing, and teachers can share this tool with students to enhance their ability to create a valuable product.

Because secondary standards often include more content, secondary teachers have to do more decision making about what to emphasize in the unpacked document's first two columns and what to add to the third column as additional information. The unpacked standard for grades 9 and 10 writing in figure 1.7 is adjustable so that teachers can have the best impact on students. For example, the first point under the standard lists various examples of what students should do to engage the reader, all of which teachers could present as additional information. However, by taking that information and listing it in the first two columns, teachers make students very aware of the recommended inclusions and the components necessary when attempting to engage the reader. Determine which placement of words will best influence student success, assuming students use the document to assist them in writing their narratives.

Content Area: English Language Arts (Writing)

Specific Standard: W.9–10.3—Write narratives to develop real or imagined experiences or events using effective technique, well-chosen details, and well-structured event sequences.
- a. Engage and orient the reader by setting out a problem, situation, or observation, establishing one or multiple point(s) of view, and introducing a narrator and/or characters; create a smooth progression of experiences or events.
- b. Use narrative techniques, such as dialogue, pacing, description, reflection, and multiple plot lines, to develop experiences, events, and/or characters.
- c. Use a variety of techniques to sequence events so that they build on one another to create a coherent whole.
- d. Use precise words and phrases, telling details, and sensory language to convey a vivid picture of the experiences, events, setting, and/or characters.
- e. Provide a conclusion that follows from and reflects on what is experienced, observed, or resolved over the course of the narrative.

Verbs or Actions	Receivers of the Actions	Additional Information (What, where, why, how, examples, teacher notes)
Engage	Reader	
Set	Problem, situation, or observation	
Establish	One or more points of view	
Introduce	Narrator or characters	
Create	Smooth progression	
Use	Narrative techniques	Like dialogue, pacing, description, reflection, and multiple plot lines

Develop	Experiences, Events, and/or Characters	
Use	Variety of techniques	To sequence To create a coherent whole
Use	Precise words, Precise phrases, and Sensory language	
Tell	Details	
Convey	Vivid picture	Of experiences, events, setting, and/or characters
Provide	Conclusion	That follows and reflects on experiences, observations, or resolutions from the narrative

Source for standard: NGA & CCSSO, 2010a.

FIGURE 1.7: Example unpacked document for Writing standard 3, grades 9–10.

Now that you have seen a few examples of the process, let's try one. Take a look at figure 1.8. How would you unpack the standard? Give it a try in the blank area of the template; a full-page reproducible version of the template also appears on page 30. There is more than one correct way to unpack most standards, so slight variations are totally acceptable. The completed document should be easy to interpret, with the key components apparent.

Content Area: English Language Arts (Reading—Literature)		
Specific Standard: RL.2.2—Recount stories, including fables and folktales from diverse cultures, and determine their central message, lesson, or moral.		
Verbs or Actions	**Receivers of the Actions**	**Additional Information** (What, where, why, how, examples, teacher notes)

Source for standard: NGA & CCSSO, 2010a.

FIGURE 1.8: Try it—Unpacked standards document template for Reading—Literature standard 2, grade 2.

When you have finished, compare your document with figure 1.9 (page 18), which shows one example of how to unpack the standard. This is an interesting standard because it has some options to consider. The special words *and* and *or* are both in the standard, which causes us to take notice of the elements of choice that are present.

Content Area: English Language Arts (Reading—Literature)

Specific Standard: RL.2.2—Recount stories, including fables and folktales from diverse cultures, and determine their central message, lesson, or moral.

Verbs or Actions	Receivers of the Actions	Additional Information (What, where, why, how, examples, teacher notes)
Recount	Stories	
Include	Fables and Folktales	From diverse cultures
Determine	Central message, lesson, or moral	

Source for standard: NGA & CCSSO, 2010a.

FIGURE 1.9: Example unpacked document for Reading—Literature standard 2, grade 2.

The standard clearly states that students are to recount stories. After that, we have a decision to make. Do we want to list *including fables and folktales* as additional information, or do we want to list it separately in order to emphasize it? Either will work; your decision depends on how obvious you want the placement to be in the unpacked document. In the example in figure 1.9, I chose to list the actions separately.

The word *and* in the standard indicates that both fables and folktales are included and students are to have experience reading a variety of both types of literature from diverse cultures. Because of this, I placed *fables* and *folktales* on separate lines in the chart to indicate that students are expected to read both.

The word *or* also appears because the standard asks students to determine the central message, lesson, or moral. Again, *or* indicates choice. To illustrate that this is the case, I placed the three items all on the same line and included the word *or* as emphasis. Students should have experience determining one or more, but the standard is not asking that students have experience with all three.

UNPACKING STANDARDS BY DOMAIN

Although I have chosen unpacking one standard at a time to illustrate the unpacking process, for ease of use in the classroom, it makes sense to unpack all standards within a domain so they are listed in one place. This makes the unpacked standards easy to locate and compare. Let's explore full domain examples for both English language arts and mathematics.

ENGLISH LANGUAGE ARTS EXAMPLE

Figure 1.10 shares a complete set of ten standards for second-grade writing, all listed within the same document. I recommend creating a series of unpacked documents, one for each category within the subject, including for Common Core English language arts, Reading: Literature, Reading: Informational Text, Reading: Foundational Skills, Writing, Speaking and Listening, and Language.

Content Area: English Language Arts (Writing)

Specific Standard: W.2.1—Write opinion pieces in which they introduce the topic or book they are writing about, state an opinion, supply reasons that support the opinion, use linking words (e.g., *because, and, also*) to connect opinion and reasons, and provide a concluding statement or section.

Verbs or Actions	Receivers of the Actions	Additional Information (What, where, why, how, examples, teacher notes)
Write	Opinion pieces	
Introduce	Topic or book	
State	Opinion	
Supply	Reasons	To support the opinion
Use	Linking words	Examples: *because, and, also*
Connect	Opinions and Reasons	
Provide	Concluding statement or section	

Specific Standard: W.2.2—Write informative/explanatory texts in which they introduce a topic, use facts and definitions to develop points, and provide a concluding statement or section.

Verbs or Actions	Receivers of the Actions	Additional Information (What, where, why, how, examples, teacher notes)
Write	Informative/explanatory texts	
Introduce	Topic	
Use	Facts and Definitions	To develop points
Provide	Concluding statement or section	

Specific Standard: W.2.3—Include details to describe actions, thoughts, and feelings, use temporal words to signal event order, and provide a sense of closure.

Verbs or Actions	Receivers of the Actions	Additional Information (What, where, why, how, examples, teacher notes)
Include	Details	
Describe	Actions, Thoughts, and Feelings	

FIGURE 1.10: Example unpacked document for all Writing standards, grade 2.

continued ▶

Verbs or Actions	Receivers of the Actions	Additional Information (What, where, why, how, examples, teacher notes)
Use	Temporal words	To signal order
Provide	Closure	

Anchor Standard: Production and Distribution of Writing

Specific Standard: W.2.4 (begins in grade 3)

Specific Standard: W.2.5—With guidance and support from adults and peers, focus on a topic and strengthen writing as needed by revising and editing.

Verbs or Actions	Receivers of the Actions	Additional Information (What, where, why, how, examples, teacher notes)
Focus	Topic	With guidance and support
Strengthen	Writing	With guidance and support
Revise	As needed	With guidance and support
Edit	As needed	With guidance and support

Specific Standard: W.2.6—With guidance and support from adults, use a variety of digital tools to produce and publish writing, including in collaboration with peers.

Verbs or Actions	Receivers of the Actions	Additional Information (What, where, why, how, examples, teacher notes)
Use	Digital tools	With guidance and support
Produce	Writing	With guidance and support
Publish	Writing	With guidance and support
Collaborate	With peers	With guidance and support

Specific Standard: W.2.7—Participate in shared research and writing projects (e.g., read a number of books on a single topic to produce a report; record science observations).

Verbs or Actions	Receivers of the Actions	Additional Information (What, where, why, how, examples, teacher notes)
Complete	Research	Example: read books, produce reports Example: record science observations
Write	Research	Example: read books, produce reports Example: record science observations

Specific Standard: W.2.8—Recall information from experiences or gather information from provided sources to answer a question.		
Verbs or Actions	**Receivers of the Actions**	**Additional Information** (What, where, why, how, examples, teacher notes)
Recall	Information	To answer questions
Or gather	Information from provided sources	To answer questions
Specific Standard: W.2.9 (begins in grade 4)		
Specific Standard: W.2.10 (begins in grade 3)		

Source for standard: NGA & CCSSO, 2010a.

In other words, by making a complete document for each individual area, you will have an entire set of unpacked documents for all of English language arts, perhaps housed in a single folder or file for the content area. These charts will provide valuable information and give teachers and students a detailed understanding of the comprehensive nature of each part of every standard. The documents will demonstrate the progression of learning at each grade level for each topic.

There are a few things to note about figure 1.10. If there is not a standard at the grade level, as with standards 4, 9, and 10, it is still listed in the chart to show at which grade level the standard begins. This helps eliminate any confusion. If a standard simply didn't appear, one might wonder whether it was an oversight.

Notice standards 5 and 6 include the information that students can meet the standards with guidance and support. It is important to include this fact in the Additional Information column. We want to be able to easily distinguish between standards that expect students to ultimately perform independently and standards in which guidance and support are acceptable.

MATHEMATICS EXAMPLES

Now that we have spent time reviewing some English language arts standards, let's take a look at mathematics. To unpack mathematics standards, or those in any content area, use the same process. As a result, there are not multiple methods or templates to learn. The process is consistent; the charts are comparable. This is an advantage for any teacher who teaches multiple subjects.

Figure 1.11 (page 22) shares the kindergarten standards for Geometry standard A. These standards are rich in content. The unpacked document assists teachers in visualizing the scope of expectations for kindergarten students in geometry. For example, kindergartners need to not only identify shapes but also describe them.

Content Area: Mathematics (Geometry)

Specific Standard: K.G.A.1—Describe objects in the environment using names of shapes, and describe the relative positions of these objects using terms such as *above, below, beside, in front of, behind,* and *next to.*

Verbs or Actions	Receivers of the Actions	Additional Information (What, where, why, how, examples, teacher notes)
Describe	Objects	In the environment
Use	Names of shapes	
Describe	Relative positions	
Use	Terms	Examples: *above, below, beside, in front of, behind, next to*

Specific Standard: K.G.A.2—Correctly name shapes regardless of their orientations or overall size.

Verbs or Actions	Receivers of the Actions	Additional Information (What, where, why, how, examples, teacher notes)
Name	Shapes	Regardless of orientation Regardless of size

Specific Standard: K.G.A.3—Identify shapes as two-dimensional (lying in a plane, "flat") or three-dimensional ("solid").

Verbs or Actions	Receivers of the Actions	Additional Information (What, where, why, how, examples, teacher notes)
Identify	Shapes	As two-dimensional As three-dimensional

Source for standard: NGA & CCSSO, 2010b.

FIGURE 1.11: Example unpacked document for all Geometry A standards, kindergarten.

The richness of information in the mathematics standards pictured in figure 1.11 is an opportunity to really dig deep. They require that teachers identify and list each component to properly determine what is being asked of students. By listing the components separately, teachers can clearly and easily view each required piece of the standard. If teachers share with the students in this format, students can see all that they will need to accomplish. The unpacked standard and chart are presented in a format similar to a checklist, which helps students gain awareness of all they must consider in order to be successful with this standard. In the chapters that follow, it will also become obvious how to use the unpacked standard to plan standards-based assessment.

Take a look at two fifth-grade mathematics standards involving fractions in figure 1.12, viewing only the unpacked sections first. Notice how the unpacked document provides a clear overview of what is expected of students when performing these standards. The document is valuable when selecting teaching resources and planning lessons. Comparing the standards to the resources will ensure that teachers are meeting the content of the standards.

Content Area: Mathematics (Number and Operations—Fractions)		

Specific Standard: 5.NF.A.1—Add and subtract fractions with unlike denominators (including mixed numbers) by replacing given fractions with equivalent fractions in such a way as to produce an equivalent sum or difference of fractions with like denominators. *For example,* $\frac{2}{3} + \frac{5}{4} = \frac{8}{12} + \frac{15}{12} = \frac{23}{12}$. *(In general,* $\frac{a}{b} + \frac{c}{d} = \frac{(ad + bc)}{bd}$.*)*

Verbs or Actions	**Receivers of the Actions**	**Additional Information** (What, where, why, how, examples, teacher notes)
Add	Fractions	With unlike denominators
Add	Mixed numbers	With unlike denominators
Subtract	Fractions	With unlike denominators
Subtract	Mixed numbers	With unlike denominators
Find	Equivalent fractions	
Produce	Equivalent sums or differences	

Specific Standard: 5.NF.A.2—Solve word problems involving addition and subtraction of fractions referring to the same whole, including cases of unlike denominators, e.g., by using visual fraction models or equations to represent the problem. Use benchmark fractions and number sense of fractions to estimate mentally and assess the reasonableness of answers. *For example, recognize an incorrect result* $\frac{2}{5} + \frac{1}{2} = \frac{3}{7}$, *by observing that* $\frac{3}{7} < \frac{1}{2}$.

Verbs or Actions	**Receivers of the Actions**	**Additional Information** (What, where, why, how, examples, teacher notes)
Solve	Addition-of-fraction word problems	Include unlike denominators. Example: using visual fraction models or equations to represent the problem
Solve	Subtraction-of-fraction word problems	Include unlike denominators. Example: using visual fraction models or equations to represent the problem
Use	Benchmark fractions and Number sense of fractions	
Assess	Reasonableness of answers	
Recognize	Incorrect result	Example: Know that the answer $\frac{2}{5} + \frac{1}{2} = \frac{3}{7}$ is inaccurate by observing that $\frac{3}{7} < \frac{1}{2}$.

Source for standard: NGA & CCSSO, 2010b.

FIGURE 1.12: Example unpacked document for Number and Operations—Fractions A standards, grade 5.

Notice also that the standards include additional information that is not in the first two columns of the unpacked document. These are examples. Example text such as this is included within the standards themselves to illustrate what the standard is asking for. The examples are not included when unpacking simply because they are not part of the global information that the standards include, but they can appear as additional information.

As we teachers become comfortable with the unpacking process, we begin to find that creating the complete documents is not difficult. The time commitment is minimal. The value of the documents is long lasting. In chapter 2 (page 31), we will add learning targets to the unpacked document; adding another column to these examples will allow us to begin thinking about how to formulate learning targets.

Charting all standards from a single topic area on one chart is beneficial because we can view all the expectations for the year in detail in one place. Comparing the writing document with the documents of all other English language arts strands will support long- and short-term planning. We can pair standards that are connected by topic or content. We can combine those that overlap. This leads to efficiency when attempting to teach so many standards within a year.

Unpacking and charting the standards support our ability to identify those standards that are essential—those that are a priority (Ainsworth, 2015). Identification of those that take priority over other standards helps us plan the time allotted to teach and assess the standards. The unpacked standard clearly indicates levels of complexity. The first column of the chart, which includes verbs and actions, indicates the rigorous expectations of the standard. For example, if the standard states that a student should be able to recall a fact, its level of rigor is less than that of standards that require students to compare, contrast, analyze, and evaluate. As a result of unpacking the standards, teachers can view the building-block nature of the standards; in other words, standards can build on each other, with some foundational ones leading to others that support lifelong learning. Teachers can identify the standards that have the greatest potential current and long-term impact, and they can adjust the length of time spent on a standard according to its level of importance. Again, this is possible because all standards are unpacked and in a single location for easy access and review.

HOW TEACHERS SHARE STANDARDS WITH STUDENTS

When teachers decide for themselves what to teach and assign, students can learn. Certainly, teachers have that ability, but students will benefit even more from knowing that the teacher has a master plan that includes standards. The learning that takes place is for the student. Consider sharing the big picture with the students so they understand the master plan. This will clarify that there are immediate goals but also a long-term outcome, the success of which depends on the pieces the students learn along the way.

It is also, of course, essential to share the learning targets derived from the standards with students so they better understand what they will know and be able to do by the end of a period of time. These targets are written in such a way that students *commit* to learning the components the standards address. Sharing the standard itself is similar to sharing the entire journey, while learning targets assist students in committing to the steps along the way. Standards help students see the master plan, while learning targets help students commit to their responsibility to succeed in learning what is stated in the master plan. Chapter 2 goes into more detail on creating learning targets and sharing them with students.

Here is an example of something you might say or hand out to students to explain standards and how you will use them throughout the school year:

- -

Students, each year in school, teachers have a plan of what they will teach throughout the year. The plan is based on standards. Standards are targets that you are expected to learn at this grade level in each subject. Standards create a road map or path that will lead to your success now and later. Each grade level has sets of standards. Teachers use them to plan how you will show what you have learned so they can be confident that you will succeed this year and in your future. Teachers create lessons and assignments to help you learn and grow. Each day, in each subject, I will identify what you are to be learning so that you know the plan for the class. Imagine that we are going on a trip during each subject. Our end destination is based on the standard we are currently learning. I want you to know where we are going with your learning. I want you to know how you will get there so you can experience success. Remember, you are learning for yourself. You are experiencing new ways to know and grow. I will be with you only this year, but what you learn will be with you forever.

- -

This example is appropriate for fourth grade up to and including secondary classrooms, perhaps with minor modifications to vocabulary. In grades K–3, the content can be much the same; again, use grade-level-appropriate vocabulary, and make sure the students understand the message. At any level, teachers can include examples and adjust vocabulary to best meet the needs of the students. Be sure to keep the focus on the complete requirements of the standard.

At this point, we can share the unpacked documents with students to help them understand what they are to accomplish. Let's use figure 1.13 as an example of how we can share learning expectations with students.

Content Area: English Language Arts (Reading—Literature)		
Specific Standard: RL.3.1—Ask and answer questions to demonstrate understanding of a text, referring explicitly to the text as the basis for the answers.		
Verbs or Actions	**Receivers of the Actions**	**Additional Information** (What, where, why, how, examples, teacher notes)
Ask	Questions	To demonstrate understanding
Answer	Questions	To demonstrate understanding
Refer	To the text	To answer questions

Source for standard: NGA & CCSSO, 2010a.

FIGURE 1.13: Example unpacked document for Reading—Literature standard 1, grade 3.

Consider sharing the last three rows of the chart with students. If the vocabulary in the standard is a bit more sophisticated than students are accustomed to, define the vocabulary if it is key to student success in future standards. Simplify the vocabulary if it is not essential to the standard itself.

Following is an example of how you could share the standard:

Students, this week, we are going to concentrate on key ideas and details in the stories you read. We will be looking for those pieces of the stories that provide us with important information. In order to achieve our standard, you will be answering questions about what you have read. When you answer questions, I will ask that you refer to the story and specifically answer the questions to show me that you understand. You will also think about what you have read to create your own questions that we will use to help us discuss key ideas and details you identified when reading the story. Do you have any questions before we begin?

Our goal in sharing the standards with students is to make the students aware of what specifically we expect them to accomplish. The unpacked standards offer a structure that helps achieve that end. This structure helps the students realize that they are responsible for their learning. It helps them know what they need to know and be able to do not only on a daily basis but also throughout the year.

Let's look at figure 1.14, which features a grade 3 English language arts standard adopted in Texas in 2017. We will again look at the vocabulary in the standard. Substituting any vocabulary should only, if at all, be necessary at the early elementary level, and then only if that language is deemed unessential to the standard.

Content Area: English Language Arts and Reading

Specific Standard: 3.b.1—Developing and sustaining foundational language skills: listening, speaking, discussion, and thinking—oral language. The student develops oral language through listening, speaking, and discussion. The student is expected to:
  a. Listen actively, ask relevant questions to clarify information, and make pertinent comments
  b. Follow, restate, and give oral instructions that involve a series of related sequences of action
  c. Speak coherently about the topic under discussion, employing eye contact, speaking rate, volume, enunciation, and the conventions of language to communicate ideas effectively
  d. Work collaboratively with others by following agreed-upon rules, norms, and protocols
  e. Develop social communication such as conversing politely in all situations

Verbs or Actions	Receivers of the Actions	Additional Information (What, where, why, how, examples, teacher notes)
Listen	Actively	
Ask	Relevant questions	
Clarify	Information	
Make	Pertinent comments	
Follow	Oral instructions	For a series of actions
Restate	Oral instructions	For a series of actions
Give	Oral instructions	For a series of actions
Speak	Coherently on the topic	

Employ	Eye contact, Speaking rate, Volume, Enunciation, and Conventions of language	
Work	Collaboratively	Following rules, norms, and protocols
Develop	Social communication skills	

Source for standard: Texas Education Agency, 2017.

FIGURE 1.14: Example unpacked document for English language arts and reading standard 1, grade 3.

Notice that the standard illustrated in figure 1.14 shows a list of student expectations that will be quite valuable to share with students. Teachers can substitute some vocabulary without impacting the intent of the standard. They can share this list with students with an explanation and some slight adjustment if desired, and they will likely do so as needed throughout the unit because all the list is unlikely to be necessary all at once. Focus on what is necessary at a point in time so as not to overwhelm or confuse students. For example, teachers might say the following:

Students, this month, we are beginning to work on some speaking and listening skills that are important to our success in school. Let's look at what the standard is telling us. First, we need to listen actively, which means that we are listening well. We know what the speaker is saying and could even share that information with others if they asked us to do so. When listening, we should be able to ask relevant questions, which means we ask questions that are directly related to what we are hearing. If there is any confusion, we want to clarify information to make sure that we understand it and that what we are hearing has a clear meaning to us. Lastly, if we comment on the information, we make pertinent comments, which means comments are related to the conversation. Any questions?

Words like *relevant* and *pertinent*, depending on grade level, may need clarification to ensure students understand expectations regarding listening, gaining information, and commenting on that information.

IN SUMMARY

We teachers unpack standards in order to best understand their contents. The unpacked documents are structured in such a way that we can also use them to easily share the standards with students. If we expect students to achieve the standards, students need to receive the information contained within the standards. We can consider it essential to their understanding of what they are learning and why they are learning it.

This chapter suggests a three-column method for unpacking standards. The method serves to illustrate individual components of each standard. The unpacked documents set the stage for next steps, and you will use the documents to create learning targets, assessments, rubrics, and more, all highlighted in future chapters.

I recommend that teachers unpack all standards for the entire content area. Divisions within the content should be unpacked in a single document. For example, in English language arts, writing standards are unpacked within a single document. This aids teachers in easily locating and reviewing the standards. If you complete the unpacking using Google Docs or a spreadsheet, for example, you can save all documents in a single content-area folder. Finding the documents will not be a problem when you organize them in a logical location and format.

Always remember to share the standards with students. Students find standards meaningful when they receive them in an easy-to-understand format at a time when they will be engaging in activities that promote learning those standards. Sharing standards is like involving students in the educational journey they are about to take; students have an easier time packing and preparing for the journey when they know where they are going and what they are expected to accomplish.

In the next chapter, we'll move on to using our unpacked documents to create learning targets.

Unpacked Standards Document

Content Area:		
Specific Standard:		
Verbs or Actions	**Receivers of the Actions**	**Additional Information** (What, where, why, how, examples, teacher notes)

Try It: Unpacked Standards Document Template for Reading—Literature Standard 2, Grade 2

Content Area: English Language Arts (Reading—Literature)		
Specific Standard: RL.2.2—Recount stories, including fables and folktales from diverse cultures, and determine their central message, lesson, or moral.		
Verbs or Actions	**Receivers of the Actions**	**Additional Information** (What, where, why, how, examples, teacher notes)

CHAPTER 2

DESIGNING STANDARDS-BASED LEARNING TARGETS

I've never been a person who wants to go on a trip to a surprise destination. I want to understand where I am going and prepare for what I am about to experience. This will help me better enjoy and understand my journey. Knowing will allow me to plan for the journey and set my expectations. What do I want to experience? What do I hope to learn and do at my destination? I believe learning in the classroom can be compared to going on a trip. Each lesson is a new adventure for students. If they have a clear understanding of where they are going, they are more likely to have a successful journey (Fisher, Frey, Amador, & Assof, 2018).

Learning targets provide students with the information they need in order to understand where they are going and what they are expected to achieve. When used in conjunction with the lesson, targets allow teachers to help students understand expectations and have a basis for self-evaluation. Students are more likely to achieve the desired outcome when they are clear on what they are to do (Moss & Brookhart, 2012).

John Hattie (2012), a renowned educator and author, writes about how important it is for students to know and understand a lesson's learning intentions. Though he doesn't use the term *learning targets*, he's referring to the same concept when he speaks of the importance of both the teacher and the students knowing what students will know as a result of the learning experience. He believes that clarity in what is to be learned increases a bond of trust between the teacher and the students (Hattie, 2012). Learning targets are intended to provide this clarity.

Standards provide the specific information that teachers will share within learning targets. Because what teachers teach in the classroom is based on the standards, and learning targets share the educational outcomes, it makes sense that there is a direct connection between the two. As a result, this chapter will discuss how to create standards-based learning targets in student-friendly language that are specific and directly related to each component of the standard. Then we'll discuss more precisely how to use learning targets with students.

HOW TO DESIGN LEARNING TARGETS

Learning targets provide students with a straightforward statement informing them of what they will achieve after learning the standard. Sometimes called *learning outcomes*, they state what students should know and be able to do by the end of a given period of time. A clear, concise target points students in the right direction. Whether posted in the classroom, shared orally, or both, learning targets prepare students for new learning. They offer students concrete expectations of what teachers expect them to accomplish.

In chapter 1 (page 9), we unpacked standards. In this chapter, we'll use the unpacked documents to design two types of learning targets: (1) overarching and (2) specific. We'll add to the unpacked standards document format you have become familiar with. Following the listed specific standard is an overarching learning target, which is quite broad and asks a lot of the students within one statement. This helps students recognize the global nature of what they will be able to do when they complete the work of the standard. In lengthy standards, the overarching standard does not include the level of detail that emerges when the standard is unpacked. This chapter adds a fourth column, Detailed Learning Targets, to the unpacked document for specific or more detailed learning targets. Detailed targets are beneficial because they are specific and can be shared with the students when they correspond with the area of concentration within the current lesson. Students will receive an exact expectation that relates to the current lesson in which they are engaged. The target for that day is defined and detailed; it is not global or overarching. A blank reproducible version of the template appears on page 43.

Figure 2.1 provides an example of the unpacked document with learning targets. The document unpacks a grade 2 Reading—Literature standard that asks students to answer *who*, *what*, *where*, *when*, *why*, and *how* questions as stated in the global learning target. The desire is to have students become comfortable asking and answering each type of question over time. Notice that the learning targets listed have the word *can* in parentheses. Although the word is sometimes used within targets, it tends to soften them. In other words, students might interpret the targets as saying, "I can do it but may or may not." It is not a strong commitment to the learning. If the word is removed, a strong statement remains, leaving no doubt as to the expectation. However, both approaches are acceptable depending on teacher and student needs, and both appear in the examples. Use what works for you.

Content Area: English Language Arts (Reading—Literature)			
Specific Standard: RL.2.1—Ask and answer such questions as *who, what, where, when, why,* and *how* to demonstrate understanding of key details in a text. **Overarching Learning Target:** I (can) ask and answer questions about what I have read, sharing key details from the book or story to show I understand.			
Verbs or Actions	**Receivers of the Actions**	**Additional Information** (What, where, why, how, examples, teacher notes)	**Detailed Learning Targets**
Ask	Questions	Who What Where When Why How	I (can) successfully ask questions about what I read. I (can) include questions about who, what, where, when, why, and how things happened within the text.
Answer	Questions	Who What Where When Why How	I (can) successfully answer questions about what I read. I (can) answer questions about who, what, where, when, why, and how things happened within the text.
Demonstrate	Understanding	Of key details	When I ask questions, I show that I understand key details in what I have read by what I ask. When I answer questions, I show that I understand key details in what I have read by how I answer.

Source for standard: NGA & CCSSO, 2010a.

FIGURE 2.1: Example unpacked document for Reading—Literature standard 1, grade 2.

To get into more detail about writing learning targets, let's look at an example unpacked kindergarten standard from Texas. Figure 2.2 highlights the unpacked document (without learning targets) while figure 2.3 (page 34) shares some learning target examples, comparing those that are OK to those that are even better.

Content Area: English Language Arts and Reading		

Specific Standard: K.2.D—Demonstrate print awareness by:
  i. Identifying the front cover, back cover, and title page of a book
  ii. Holding a book right side up, turning pages correctly, and knowing that reading moves from top to bottom and left to right with return sweep
  iii. Recognizing that sentences are comprised of words separated by spaces and recognizing word boundaries
  iv. Recognizing the difference between a letter and a printed word
  v. Identifying all uppercase and lowercase letters		

Verbs or Actions	**Receivers of the Actions**	**Additional Information** (What, where, why, how, examples, teacher notes)
Demonstrate	Print awareness	

FIGURE 2.2: Example unpacked document for English language arts and reading standard 2.D, kindergarten.

continued ▶

Verbs or Actions	Receivers of the Actions	Additional Information (What, where, why, how, examples, teacher notes)
Identify	Front cover, Back cover, and Title page	Of a book
Hold	Book	Right side up
Turn	Pages	Correctly
Know	Reading moves from top to bottom and Reading moves from left to right	
Recognize	Sentences are made from words and Words are separated by spaces	
Recognize	The difference between a letter and a word	
Identify	All uppercase letters and All lowercase letters	

Source for standard: Texas Education Agency, 2017.

OK Learning Target	Better Learning Target
I can demonstrate print awareness.	I can show that I understand print is organized in ways that help me as I learn to read.
I can identify the front cover of the book.	I can find and show someone the front cover of any book.
I can identify the back cover of the book.	I can find and show someone the back cover of any book.
I can identify the title of the book.	I can locate and show someone the title page of any book.
I hold the book right side up.	I know which way to hold a book so that it is right side up and words are in the right direction.
I know that reading moves from top to bottom.	I know that the words on the page of a book are read from top to bottom, and I can show what that means by pointing to the page of the book.
I know that reading moves from left to right.	I know that the words on the page of a book are read from left to right, and I can show what that means by pointing to the page of the book.
I recognize that sentences are made from words.	I know that sentences are made from words, and I can point to words in a sentence.
I recognize that words are separated by spaces.	I know that words are separated by spaces, and I can point to those spaces in a sentence.
I recognize the difference between a letter and a word.	I know the difference between a letter and a word, and I can tell anyone what the difference is.
I can identify all uppercase letters.	I know each uppercase letter of the alphabet and can correctly point each out when asked.
I can identify all lowercase letters.	I know each lowercase letter of the alphabet and can correctly point each out when asked.

FIGURE 2.3: Example learning targets derived from English language arts and reading standard 2.D, kindergarten.

Each example learning target in figure 2.3 is based, line by line, on the unpacked standard in figure 2.2. The first column is mostly taken word for word from the standard, which creates a great explanation for the teacher and a good list for the students. The second column attempts to put a little more definition in the learning target, highlighting the performance expectation as much as possible. For example, by simply adding a brief statement to the first target, we teachers can help students know print awareness is all about understanding that books are organized in a way that helps them read. As you create targets, think about your students and what will help them best understand the expectations of the standards. You can accomplish this by using the exact words from the standards, or in some cases, you may want to add a bit to further explain the expectations.

Figure 2.4 shares a third-grade mathematics example. Notice the standard has been unpacked using the process explained in chapter 1 (page 9). The overarching and detailed learning targets have been added. In all cases, the wording of the standard has been used to create the targets.

Content Area: Mathematics (Number and Operations—Fractions)

Specific Standard: 3.NF.A.3.D—Compare two fractions with the same numerator or the same denominator by reasoning about their size. Recognize that comparisons are valid only when the two fractions refer to the same whole. Record the results of comparisons with the symbols >, =, <, and justify the conclusions.

Overarching Learning Target: I accurately compare two fractions with the same numerator or denominator using the symbols <, >, or = to compare the size of the fractions.

Verbs or Actions	Receivers of the Actions	Additional Information (What, where, why, how, examples, teacher notes)	Detailed Learning Targets
Compare	Fractions	With the same numerator With the same denominator	I accurately compare the size of fractions with the same numerator. I accurately compare the size of fractions with the same denominator.
Reason	About size		I use the size of the fractions to reason and determine which is larger, determine which is smaller, or know they are equal in size.
Recognize	The fractions refer to the same whole		When I compare fractions, I know they are part of the same whole.
Record	Results		I record the results of my comparison.
Use	<, >, =		I accurately use the symbols <, >, or = to record my findings.

Source for standard: NGA & CCSSO, 2010b.

FIGURE 2.4: Example unpacked document for Number and Operations—Fractions standard 3, grade 3.

Figure 2.4 (page 35) places each action word from the standard in a separate cell to complete the unpacking of the standard. This itemizes each action the student takes when comparing two fractions. The goal is to ensure that each portion of the standard is addressed, sharing both the overarching and the detailed learning targets.

Figure 2.5 is a mathematics example from the Texas Essential Knowledge and Skills standards for grade 4. Note that in this example, I suggest adding the words *one billion* even though the number 1,000,000,000 appears in the standard. I include this to ensure that the students know the number name and realize the expectation of comparing and ordering numbers. The clarifying words accurately and simply emphasize that students are expected to not only perform the standard but also do it correctly. As with other examples, the learning target aligns with each component of the unpacked standard, providing students with detailed expectations of what it will take to successfully meet the standard.

Content Area: Mathematics (Number and Operations)			
Specific Standard: 4.2.C—Compare and order whole numbers to 1,000,000,000 and represent comparisons using the symbols >,<, or =. **Overarching Learning Target:** I compare and order whole numbers to one billion using the >, <, and = symbols.			
Verbs or Actions	**Receivers of the Actions**	**Additional Information** (What, where, why, how, examples, teacher notes)	**Detailed Learning Targets**
Compare	Whole numbers	To 1,000,000,000	I (can) accurately compare numbers to one billion showing if a number is larger than, smaller than, or equal to another.
Order	Whole numbers	To 1,000,000,000	I (can) accurately place numbers up to one billion in order from smallest to largest or largest to smallest.
Use	>, <, =	For comparisons	I (can) compare numbers to one billion accurately using the signs >, <, or =.

Source for standard: Texas Education Agency, 2017.

FIGURE 2.5: Example unpacked document for Mathematics (Number and Operations) standard 2.C, grade 4.

Figure 2.6 provides another example in mathematics. This example gives students a clear understanding of what they are to know and do when making measurements. It becomes clear to students that they need to choose the correct tool and unit when completing a variety of measurements.

Content Area: Mathematics (Numeracy, Measurement, and Other Applications of Shape and Space)			
Specific Standard: Choose the best measuring tool and unit to measure the capacity, volume, mass, or surface area of specific objects (e.g., volume of air in classroom, capacity of a pill bottle, mass of a train full of wheat, surface area of a kitchen table). **Overarching Learning Target:** I use the best tool and unit when measuring the capacity, volume, mass, or surface area of objects.			
Verbs or Actions	**Receivers of the Actions**	**Additional Information** (What, where, why, how, examples, teacher notes)	**Detailed Learning Targets**
Choose	Tool	For measurement	I choose the correct tool when measuring a variety of shapes.
Choose	Unit	For measurement	I choose the correct unit when measuring a variety of shapes.
Measure	Volume, mass, or surface area	Of specific objects	I correctly use the tools and units when measuring volume, mass, and surface area.

Source for standard: Government of British Columbia, 2020.

FIGURE 2.6: Example unpacked document for a Canadian standard for numeracy, measurement, and other applications of shape and space.

Figure 2.7 shares another mathematics example to illustrate the method for learning targets for a seventh-grade standard.

Content Area: Mathematics (Geometry)			
Specific Standard: 7.G.B.6—Solve real-world and mathematical problems involving area, volume, and surface area of two- and three-dimensional objects composed of triangles, quadrilaterals, polygons, cubes, and right prisms. **Overarching Learning Target:** I solve real-world and mathematical problems involving area, volume, and surface area of two- and three-dimensional objects composed of triangles, quadrilaterals, polygons, cubes, and right prisms.			
Verbs or Actions	**Receivers of the Actions**	**Additional Information** (What, where, why, how, examples, teacher notes)	**Detailed Learning Targets**
Solve	Real-world problems		I solve real-world problems using area, volume, and surface area.
Solve	Mathematical problems		I solve mathematical problems using area, volume, and surface area.

FIGURE 2.7: Example unpacked document for Geometry standard 6, grade 7. continued ▶

Verbs or Actions	Receivers of the Actions	Additional Information (What, where, why, how, examples, teacher notes)	Detailed Learning Targets
Involve	Area	Of two-dimensional objects composed of triangles, quadrilaterals, polygons, cubes, and right prisms Of three-dimensional objects composed of triangles, quadrilaterals, polygons, cubes, and right prisms	I solve real-world problems and mathematical problems involving area of two-dimensional objects composed of triangles, quadrilaterals, polygons, cubes, and right prisms. I solve real-world and mathematical problems involving area of three-dimensional objects composed of triangles, quadrilaterals, polygons, cubes, and right prisms.
Involve	Volume	Of two-dimensional objects composed of triangles, quadrilaterals, polygons, cubes, and right prisms Of three-dimensional objects composed of triangles, quadrilaterals, polygons, cubes, and right prisms	I solve real-world problems and mathematical problems involving volume of two-dimensional objects composed of triangles, quadrilaterals, polygons, cubes, and right prisms. I solve real-world and mathematical problems involving volume of three-dimensional objects composed of triangles, quadrilaterals, polygons, cubes, and right prisms.
Involve	Surface area	Of two-dimensional objects composed of triangles, quadrilaterals, polygons, cubes, and right prisms Of three-dimensional objects composed of triangles, quadrilaterals, polygons, cubes, and right prisms	I solve real-world problems and mathematical problems involving surface area of two-dimensional objects composed of triangles, quadrilaterals, polygons, cubes, and right prisms. I solve real-world and mathematical problems involving surface area of three-dimensional objects composed of triangles, quadrilaterals, polygons, cubes, and right prisms.

Source for standard: NGA & CCSSO, 2010b.

Note that the overarching learning target is the standard itself. This reminds us teachers that although students need to know the individual pieces of the standard, they should be aware that all pieces are part of a single standard. The unpacked standard clearly illustrates the number of expectations in the standard. The students are to solve both real-world and mathematical problems involving area, volume, and surface area using a variety of two- and three-dimensional shapes. The standard doesn't offer choices of doing some and not others, which is indicated by the use of the word *and* four times within the standard. The learning targets share with students both global and specific information about what they are to accomplish.

Learning targets in the area of writing provide students with all they need to consider when successfully completing a writing standard. Figure 2.8 provides a look at a sixth-grade Common Core Writing standard.

Content Area: English Language Arts (Writing)

Specific Standard: W.6.2—Write informative/explanatory texts to examine a topic and convey ideas, concepts, and information through the selection, organization, and analysis of relevant content.
   a. Introduce a topic; organize ideas, concepts, and information, using strategies such as definition, classification, comparison/contrast, and cause/effect; include formatting (e.g., headings), graphics (e.g., charts, tables), and multimedia when useful to aiding comprehension.
   b. Develop the topic with relevant facts, definitions, concrete details, quotations, or other information and examples.
   c. Use appropriate transitions to clarify the relationships among ideas and concepts.
   d. Use precise language and domain-specific vocabulary to inform about or explain the topic.
   e. Establish and maintain a formal style.
   f. Provide a concluding statement or section that follows from the information or explanation presented.

Overarching Learning Target: I write informative texts to explain a topic and share ideas and information by selecting, organizing, and analyzing relevant content.

Verbs or Actions	Receivers of the Actions	Additional Information (What, where, why, how, examples, teacher notes)	Detailed Learning Targets
Introduce	Topic		I clearly introduce the information to be presented.
Organize	Ideas, Concepts, and Information	Using definition, classification, comparison, and contrast	I organize the ideas, concepts, and information in my writing. I use definitions, classifications, comparison, and contrast to help readers understand.
Include	Formatting, Graphics, and Multimedia	When useful	I include headings, graphics, and multimedia when they are useful to my presentation.
Develop	Topic	With facts, definitions, details, quotations, and examples	I develop the topic using facts, definitions, details, quotations, and examples as appropriate to my writing.
Use	Transitions	To clarify relationships among ideas and concepts	I use transitions to relate ideas and concepts in my writing.
Use	Precise and domain-specific vocabulary	To inform about or explain the topic	I choose precise and domain-specific vocabulary in my writing to best inform about and explain the topic.
Establish	A formal style		I establish and maintain a formal style in my writing.
Maintain	A formal style		
Provide	Concluding section or statement	That follows from the information or explanation presented	I provide a conclusion in my writing that follows from the information or explanation presented.

Source for standard: NGA & CCSSO, 2010a.

FIGURE 2.8: Example unpacked document for Writing standard 2, grade 6.

The first three columns share the unpacked standard and supply a visually pleasing checklist of all components of the standard. This chart assists students in recalling the important components of writing. The Detailed Learning Targets column shares detailed expectations of the standard.

This combination provides clarity and transparent expectations. When learning targets and unpacked documents are combined, students should have little doubt about their role in demonstrating their understanding of the standard. As you review figure 2.8 (page 39), pay particular attention to the information it provides to students. Notice that the wording of the learning targets is taken directly from the standard and stated as actions that the students will complete.

The vocabulary of the standards is important for the students to understand, as it will be used repeatedly throughout the year and beyond. When it is used and unfamiliar to the students, define it for clarity, and include it in the unpacked standard and the learning targets. In chapter 1, we saw a standard that uses the word *recount*, asking students to recount a story (see figure 1.8, page 17). This word might be unfamiliar to the students. The learning target could read, "I accurately recount, or retell, stories using details from the story." This statement honors the vocabulary used within the standard and gives students further clarity if they are unfamiliar with the terminology.

HOW TO USE THE TARGETS WITH STUDENTS

Many schools ask teachers to post learning targets daily. Posting them is simply not enough. If students are to internalize and take ownership of targets, teachers must ensure students can do all three of the following.

1. Be aware of the targets.

2. Understand the targets.

3. Make the connection between the tasks they are completing and what the targets state.

Figure 2.9 displays a Common Core Speaking and Listening standard.

Content Area: English Language Arts (Speaking and Listening)			
Specific Standard: SL.3.4—Report on a topic or text, tell a story, or recount an experience with appropriate facts and relevant, descriptive details, speaking clearly at an understandable pace. **Overarching Learning Target:** I clearly report on topics, including appropriate facts and details, using an understandable pace.			
Verbs or Actions	**Receivers of the Actions**	**Additional Information** (What, where, why, how, examples, teacher notes)	**Detailed Learning Targets**
Report	Topic or text Story		I report on topics, texts, or stories.
Recount	Experience		I recount experiences.
Use	Appropriate facts, Relevant details, and Descriptive details		When reporting, I use appropriate facts and relevant and descriptive details.
Speak	Clearly		When reporting, I speak clearly.
Use	Understandable pace		When I report, my pace can be understood by my audience.

Source for standard: NGA & CCSSO, 2010a.

FIGURE 2.9: Example unpacked document for Speaking and Listening standard 4, grade 3.

A learning target in the figure states, "When reporting, I use appropriate facts and relevant and descriptive details." Consider introducing it using the wording that follows:

Students, today, we are concentrating on our Speaking and Listening standard. More specifically, you will be preparing to report to your classmates on a topic, a text that you have read, or a story of your choice. You get to decide. The learning target we are specifically working on today states, "When reporting, I use appropriate facts and relevant and descriptive details." This means that after you decide what you are going to talk to us about, you need to decide what facts are important to help us understand. You will identify details that are relevant to the topic and important to develop your reporting. You will also want to add descriptive details to bring your report to life and engage the interest of those listening to you. If you do these things, your audience will understand and feel engaged in the topic you have chosen when you share it with them. Before we continue, what questions do you have about our learning target today?

When speaking with the students about the learning target, identify where it is posted in the room so students will be able to refer to it as they are developing their report.

In the chapters that follow, most figures, including unpacked documents, will feature examples of learning targets.

IN SUMMARY

Learning targets assist students in understanding the standards. A direct connection between the standard and the learning target creates a direct link between what the teacher is teaching and the performance expected from the student. Learning is purposeful, and expectations are clear.

Although, on occasion, language within the standard may be sophisticated for the grade level, the teacher should use the language if it directly relates to the standard's expectation. For example, if the standard asks students to state an opinion, the word *opinion* should appear in the learning target and be defined and clarified with examples so students understand it. The vocabulary in the standard builds on the previous year, and content-specific words are commonly used across grade levels, so teaching students the language of the standards will benefit them as they progress through the grades.

I recommend adding the learning targets to the standards document as illustrated in this chapter so there is a direct connection between each portion of the unpacked document and each learning target. Each piece necessary to successfully complete the standard is present so the big picture is obvious. Yet each piece is not isolated. Isolation of individual learning targets can lead to a lack of understanding as to how the pieces are related to the whole. After figure 2.9, for example, you considered how you would talk to students about one piece of the standard, yet having the entire standard present in the unpacked document helps students realize that they are not just finding details to add to their report; the ultimate goal is verbally sharing the report with others. The overarching target is helpful in making students aware of the big picture. The individual learning targets assist students in creating a pathway to achieve the overarching learning target, thereby achieving the standard.

In the next chapter, we will continue to use the unpacked document, including the learning targets, to build assessments that are based on and associated with the standards we teachers use.

Unpacked Standards Document With Learning Targets

Content Area:			
Specific Standard:			
Overarching Learning Target:			
Verbs or Actions	**Receivers of the Actions**	**Additional Information** (What, where, why, how, examples, teacher notes)	**Detailed Learning Targets**

PART 2

TOOLS AND ANALYSIS

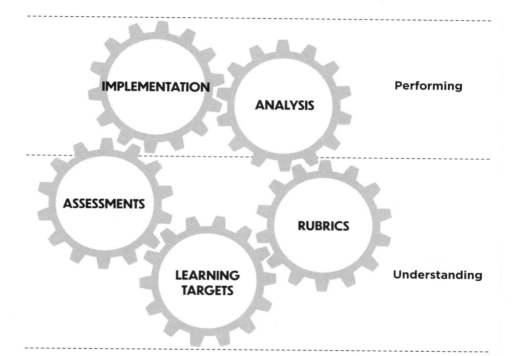

Chapters 3 and 4 highlight the tools to use to evaluate student performance. Chapter 3 discusses quality assessment design and implementation. Chapter 4 considers the benefits of rubrics as well as rubric design.

Chapters 5 and 6 are dedicated to gathering and evaluating assessment results. Chapter 5 shares the benefits of common assessment implementation and provides crucial considerations for prior to, during, and after implementation. Chapter 6 is devoted to gathering, displaying, and analyzing student data.

All four chapters continue to support the use of standards as the basis for both the tools and the analysis process.

CHAPTER 3

CREATING STANDARDS-BASED ASSESSMENTS

I find assessment design to be an interesting experience, sometimes even a dilemma. Do I rely solely on existing resources? Do I look for assessments online that match what I'm teaching? Do I design assessments myself? Do I work with a collaborative team to design them? (I will go into much more detail about collaborating to create common assessments in chapter 5, page 83.) Basically, we teachers are looking for items that match the components discovered in the unpacked standard. So, what's the best way to identify the assessment? Any or all of the methods I've mentioned. The match is what is important. Review the items. Find the perfect match. Frankly, at times, I feel that designing your own assessment is most efficient, yet some teachers feel most secure identifying an existing resource. No matter the path you take, alignment of the standard's components and the assessment items is essential.

No matter the assessment type, frequency, or length, the purpose of assessments should always be the same: determining whether students can adequately demonstrate understanding of the components of the standards. The reasons for using the assessments and their length may differ. The length of the assessments should be appropriate for what is being assessed, and the frequency should be determined by student performance and the teacher's need for data to consider next steps.

Tests identified or designed by teachers can prove to be formative and improve student learning. Standards-based assessments play an important role in student success. Assessments assist teachers in gathering information to make good instructional decisions based on evidence (Stiggins, 2005, 2014).

In this chapter, we'll discuss some important considerations for assessment design—beginning with the unpacked standards document, identifying the required level of rigor, and determining the content of the assessment—all illustrated with numerous examples.

ASSESSMENT DESIGN

For the purposes of this book, *assessments* are defined as exhibits, samples, or examples of student performance that are created and evaluated to compare student results to the expectations of one or more standards or learning targets within a standard. An assessment should provide students with opportunities to show their expertise on a standard or a portion of a standard. Multiple assessments provide the data that create a well-rounded picture of students' performance and understanding of the grade-level standards.

Assessment results form a foundation for next steps and support teachers in their ability to respond as needed. Because the tasks within the assessment are directly tied to the standard, the assessment results will give teachers a clear understanding of what students know and what they are struggling with.

When building an assessment, as always, start with the standard, and determine which learning target or targets the assessment will encompass. Remember to include all aspects of the learning target within the assessment. We teachers want to make sure we eventually assess all components in the unpacked document, but let's also keep in mind that the individual components have a larger purpose as outlined in the overarching learning target. We assess the pieces (the detailed learning targets) while making sure that students are able to perform the whole expectation. We can design or identify multiple assessments so that we eventually assess the entire standard. Less sophisticated standards likely require fewer assessments than more sophisticated standards do. The number of assessments needed should be determined by the data teachers require to have confidence that the students have mastered the standard.

When designing a standards-based assessment, consider these three steps.

1. **Begin with the unpacked standards document:** In each chapter, we always get started with the unpacked documents and use them as the basis of the next step. These documents are the foundation of everything we do not just in a chapter but in a unit and a school year. The standards document is essential to every aspect of the learning process in a truly standards-based system.

2. **Identify the required level of rigor:** The assessment's level of rigor needs to match the level of rigor required in the standard. Without that match, the assessment becomes too simple or too rigorous. In order to accomplish a perfect fit, review the verbs listed in the unpacked document. If the verbs ask students to remember or identify, the skills are at a lower level, and a matching, fill-in-the-blank, or simple multiple-choice test will suffice. If the verbs ask students to analyze or compare, students will need to do a type of performance that will cause them to think at a deeper level. The assessment could have students provide short answers, demonstrate their understanding through an explanation, or respond to questions designed to encourage cognitive complexity.

3. **Design the assessment:** If the standard identifies process and not content, the content of the assessment is up to the teacher, team, school, or district. Standards for reading, writing, and speaking and listening lack content but are rich in process. To assess these standards, the assessment designers will need to identify the literature and content prior to developing the assessment. If the school or district has identified content to coincide with the standards, this has already been accomplished. If not, there is

classroom and grade-level flexibility. Mathematics standards typically identify content, and the created or identified problems will need to assess that content.

The following sections contain a variety of examples that clarify these considerations. They also touch on the possibility of identifying existing assessments.

BEGIN WITH THE UNPACKED STANDARDS DOCUMENT

Figure 3.1 is an example of an English language arts unpacked document. It features W.K.1, which is a kindergarten Common Core Writing standard in the domain of Text Types and Purposes.

Content Area: English Language Arts (Writing)

Specific Standard: W.K.1—Use a combination of drawing, dictating, and writing to compose opinion pieces in which they tell a reader the topic or the name of the book they are writing about and state an opinion or preference about the topic or book (e.g., *My favorite book is . . .*).

Overarching Learning Target: Through the use of drawing, dictating, and writing, I share my opinion about a topic or book.

Verbs or Actions	Receivers of the Actions	Additional Information (What, where, why, how, examples, teacher notes)	Detailed Learning Targets
Use	Combination	Of drawing, dictating, and writing	I use drawing to tell my opinion. I use dictating to tell my opinion. I write to tell my opinion.
Compose	Opinion or preference	About the topic or book	I use drawing, dictating, and writing to tell my opinion about a book. I use drawing, dictating, and writing to tell my opinion about a topic.

Source for standard: NGA & CCSSO, 2010a.

FIGURE 3.1: Example unpacked document for Writing standard 1, kindergarten.

In order to begin developing an assessment, teachers review the unpacked document, specifically the expectations for students. The standard in figure 3.1 asks students to draw, dictate, and write, which means that the assessment should include a combination of all three. Teachers may choose to identify an exact task to complete for the expectation, or they may decide to incorporate student choice into the assessment; for standard W.K.1, students could choose the topic or book they write about to state their opinion or preference. When deciding whether choice is appropriate, consider the age of the students, the time available for the assessment, and how long the students have had to master the standard. Although choices can empower students, having too many choices can confuse them or cause them concern. Students are less likely to fully commit to the final choice they make when they are offered too many choices (Maimaran, 2017).

The assessment in figure 3.2 (page 50), which is based on the unpacked standard in figure 3.1, creates a happy medium by including but also limiting choice. On this assessment, students have the option to add a reason for their opinion; this is part of a grade 1 standard. (The next section, page 50, provides additional information regarding rigor.)

Specific Learning Target Assessed: I use drawing, dictating, and writing to tell my opinion about a topic.

Students can choose to express their opinion about rainy days or chocolate cake.
In order to demonstrate understanding, students will:
- Name the topic of their opinion
- Draw a picture related to the topic and their opinion
- Write to express their opinion below the picture
- Dictate any additional details they would like to mention

Optional: Students can choose to add a reason for their opinion.

Source for standard: NGA & CCSSO, 2010a.

FIGURE 3.2: Example assessment for Writing standard 1, kindergarten.

The assessment in figure 3.2 includes all that the standard asks for related to an opinion about a topic. Teachers should take care to choose only topics that students are familiar with so the students actually have a choice between the topics. Teachers can also design a similar assessment asking students to state an opinion about a book. In this case, the students can receive the name of the book or a choice of books on which to form an opinion. These books might be ones the students have read or books the teacher has read to the students. Immediately before the assessment, the teacher could read the book used in the assessment to the class. In addition to these suggestions, consider other options that will best meet your needs. Because this standard uses *or* in the phrase "the topic or book," assessing both is optional.

IDENTIFY THE REQUIRED LEVEL OF RIGOR

The standard in figure 3.1 (page 49) asks students to demonstrate that they understand the book or topic and then to determine their opinion or preference about the book or topic. Two common tools can assist teachers in evaluating a standard's level of rigor. First, Bloom's (1954) taxonomy shares six levels of rigor. Second, Webb's (2002) Depth of Knowledge describes four levels of cognitive demand. Both frameworks can help us categorize standards' levels of rigor or demand by comparing the standards' expectations to the framework. This categorization practice supports the development of assessments and questions that reflect the designated level of rigor.

I further discuss both frameworks in my book *Raising the Rigor* (Depka, 2017). For even more in-depth consideration, see *Deconstructing Depth of Knowledge: A Method and Model for Deeper Teaching and Learning* (Francis, 2022) and *How to Use Bloom's Taxonomy in the Classroom: The Complete Guide* (Gershon, 2018). These two resources apply the latest thinking to the classic frameworks and offer invaluable insight for readers who wish to delve more deeply into their use. For this book's purposes, this section will give you a way to start using one or both frameworks in your assessment design.

The standard in figure 3.1 asks students only to state an opinion or preference. In first grade, students are also asked to provide a reason for the opinion and a sense of closure. Although that's not part of the kindergarten expectation, kindergartners likely have a reason for their opinion and could confidently state it. This is something teachers can ask for in the assessment to add rigor to the task; however, since it is not a grade-level expectation, it's optional. If a kindergarten student does not provide a reason, it should not reflect poorly on the student's ability to state the opinion, and it should have no impact on a report card evaluation.

The verbs and actions in the first column of the unpacked document can indicate the necessary rigor within the assessment. Should the assessment include rigorous tasks? Is a traditional list of factual questions appropriate? Is a combination of the two a better option? A task gives students the opportunity to actively engage in a process or create a product. For example, a task might ask students to identify the verbs in a sentence, or it might ask them to list five verbs that describe actions they engage in during the day. The latter task demonstrates that students understand what a verb is and requires more thinking and engagement on their part. The assessment result should clearly signify students' understanding of the expectations of the standard.

Teachers can use Bloom's taxonomy to develop assessments that have a balance of rigor. They can use Webb's Depth of Knowledge to evaluate the cognitive demand of standards and to evaluate existing assessment questions. Both methods are valuable in assessment development. Some districts choose to use one or the other. If the choice is yours, use the one that best meets your needs. Let's consider how you can use each, starting with Bloom's taxonomy, and then discuss how to ensure rigor in assessment design.

USING BLOOM'S TAXONOMY

Figure 3.3 provides information regarding the six levels in the cognitive domain of Bloom's (1954) taxonomy. The first column briefly describes each level. The second column contributes verbs that may indicate the level of cognition expected of students. For example, if students are asked to label locations on a map, that activity requires students to perform at the *remembering* level of Bloom's. If students are asked to defend an opinion on a given topic, they must perform at the *evaluating* or *creating* level of the taxonomy. In an effort to create an assessment with a balance of rigor, use Bloom's taxonomy to ensure that you design questions or tasks at various levels of cognition.

Creating (Produce something original or recreate something known.)	construct, create, design, develop, devise, extrapolate, generate, illustrate an idea, improve, judge, produce
Evaluating ↑ (Make judgments based on evidence.)	criticize, decide, defend, discover the relationship, evaluate, explain the difference, interpret, judge, justify, predict, prove
Analyzing ↑ (Relate parts to the whole, break apart information to investigate.)	analyze, categorize, classify, compare, confirm, contrast, diagram, disprove, identify the pattern, illustrate a concept, infer, outline, prove, simplify
Applying ↑ (Use information in various situations.)	calculate, compare, contrast, convert, demonstrate, determine, elaborate, solve
Understanding ↑ (Make meaning of information.)	clarify, demonstrate, describe, detail, expand, explain, express, retell, summarize
Remembering ↑ (Access knowledge from memory.)	define, describe, identify, label, list, match, memorize, name, remember, recall, recite, record, repeat, reproduce, select, state

Source: Adapted from Depka, 2017, p. 30.

FIGURE 3.3: Verbs associated with the cognitive domain of Bloom's taxonomy.

Teachers should take care to ensure the chosen verb indicates the rigor that they desire the task to have. Consider these two examples: (1) students must explain the difference in two characters' reactions to an event in the story, and (2) students must provide previously discussed information to explain the difference in two characters' reactions to an event in the story. The first example is truly asking students to perform a task at the evaluating level of Bloom's taxonomy. The second example is simply asking students to remember something previously discussed, which is a much lower-level skill.

Figure 3.4 contains an unpacked standard for which we will build an assessment using Bloom's taxonomy as a resource. This second-grade mathematics standard asks that students recognize, draw, and identify shapes.

Content Area: Mathematics (Geometry)

Specific Standard: 2.G.A.1—Recognize and draw shapes having specified attributes, such as a given number of angles or a given number of equal faces. Identify triangles, quadrilaterals, pentagons, hexagons, and cubes.
Overarching Learning Target: I recognize and draw shapes when I am aware of their specific attributes or characteristics.

Verbs or Actions	Receivers of the Actions	Additional Information (What, where, why, how, examples, teacher notes)	Detailed Learning Targets
Recognize	Shapes	With specified attributes	I recognize and can name shapes with specific attributes, like the number of sides or angles they have.
Draw	Shapes	With specified attributes	I draw and can name shapes with specific attributes, like the number of sides or angles they have.
Identify	Triangles, Quadrilaterals, Pentagons, Hexagons, and Cubes		I identify a variety of shapes by name, including triangles, quadrilaterals, pentagons, hexagons, and cubes.

Source for standard: NGA & CCSSO, 2010b.

FIGURE 3.4: Example unpacked document for Geometry standard 1, grade 2.

The action verbs within the standard indicate that students need to recognize, draw, and identify. Recognizing shapes and identifying shapes are at the remembering or understanding level of Bloom's. If we choose to add rigor, the assessment questions can ask students to choose a specific shape out of a group of shapes. This addition increases the questions' level of rigor because the students need to apply their knowledge of all shapes to choose the correct response. Drawing shapes is at least at an applying level, but by varying what we ask, we can make the level of rigor higher. Figure 3.5 provides an example assessment for the standard.

Recognizing Shapes

Name the shapes described in the following prompts.

1. A shape with exactly three angles: _____

2. Every shape with four sides: _____

3. Name and draw a three-sided shape: _____

4. Name and draw a shape with four angles: _____

5. Name and draw a shape with eight sides: _____

6. Name and draw a shape with six equal faces: _____

FIGURE 3.5: Example assessment for Geometry standard 1, grade 2.

Notice that figure 3.5 identifies shapes in different ways so that students use different pieces of information within the standard to complete the task. Although numbers 3 through 6 all ask students to "name and draw," the different descriptions incorporate the words *sides*, *angles*, and *faces*, so students need to know the shapes as well as understand the shapes' characteristics and apply them by drawing. These combinations can add rigor and also help teachers determine whether students clearly understand all aspects of the standard.

Next, let's look at an English language arts standard and compare the verbs in the unpacked standard to the tasks students will need to perform within an assessment. Figure 3.6 (page 54) shares the expectations for grade 5 students when reading informational text. Again, we will build the assessment based on those expectations. The procedure doesn't vary. The system stays the same. We start with the unpacked standards document and use its contents as a floor plan or road map with which to build the assessment.

Content Area: English Language Arts (Reading—Informational Text)

Specific Standard: RI.5.2—Determine two or more main ideas of a text and explain how they are supported by key details; summarize the text.

Overarching Learning Target: When I summarize, I determine main ideas and explain how the key details support the main ideas.

Verbs or Actions	Receivers of the Actions	Additional Information (What, where, why, how, examples, teacher notes)	Detailed Learning Targets
Determine	Main ideas	At least two	I determine the main ideas when reading for information.
Explain	How main ideas are supported	By key details	I explain how the key details support the main ideas.
Summarize	Text		I summarize the text using the main ideas.

Source for standard: NGA & CCSSO, 2010a.

FIGURE 3.6: Example unpacked document for Reading—Informational Text standard 2, grade 5.

We want students to determine, explain, and summarize. We develop or identify lessons to directly address the content of the standard. Prior to taking an assessment, students need multiple chances to demonstrate that they understand what a main idea is. They should also have practice identifying key details from the text that support the main ideas. We should assign students practice opportunities so that they see the connections among the main ideas, the supporting details, and the roles they play in summarizing the text. Main ideas are the foundation of any summary. Before students complete a global assessment of the standard, we want to feel confident that they understand all of the standard's components so they have the greatest chance of success.

To assess this standard, we'll use a graphic organizer that we can reuse throughout the year when we assess this standard. Because it is generic in nature, this graphic organizer (figure 3.7) can be used with any informational text. Its structure ensures that the contents of the standard are addressed. We can adjust (add or subtract) the number of main ideas in the graphic organizer to reflect the sophistication of the text. A reproducible version of this figure is available on page 66 for teachers who wish to use it themselves.

Read the informational text provided. Then complete the graphic organizer with the information you have learned.
List main idea 1.
List the key details that support main idea 1.
List main idea 2.
List the key details that support main idea 2.

List main idea 3.	
List the key details that support main idea 3.	
Use the main ideas and key details that you have listed to write a summary of the information.	

FIGURE 3.7: Graphic organizer assessment for reading an informational text.

If we compare the assessment in figure 3.7 to Bloom's taxonomy, we see that defining main ideas and key details is at the remembering level. To complete this assessment and show mastery of this standard, however, students need to perform at a much more rigorous level. They need to analyze the text to locate the main ideas, then evaluate the text to locate the supportive details for the main ideas they have chosen. The assessment should, as much as possible, match the expectation of rigor within the standard. For students who require more support, we could also slightly reduce the level of rigor by having students choose the main ideas and supporting details from lists made available to the students. Students would review the lists and identify all main ideas and supporting details that accurately reflect the content they have read.

USING WEBB'S DEPTH OF KNOWLEDGE

Webb's (2002) Depth of Knowledge (DOK; Francis, 2022) is designed to evaluate the cognitive demand within a standard, which we can then apply to a question or task. DOK has four levels, which are each described in table 3.1.

TABLE 3.1: Depth of Knowledge Levels and Characteristics

DOK Level	Characteristics
Level 1: Recall and Reproduction	Students recall or reproduce information or carry out a known procedure.
Level 2: Skills and Concepts	Students use information or conceptual knowledge to solve a problem. Often two or more steps are necessary to complete a task.
Level 3: Strategic Thinking	Students reason and develop a plan that will lead to a solution. Multiple steps or sources are an indication of the need for strategic thinking. There may be multiple answers to a problem.
Level 4: Extended Thinking	Students think and investigate over time. Students need to review multiple facets of a problem.

Source: Depka, 2017, p. 31; Webb, 2002.

With DOK in mind, look at the unpacked standard in figure 3.8 (page 56). The verb *recount* indicates that questions or tasks for the standard would be at DOK level 1, which encompasses recall of information. However, the second part of the standard asks students to determine a central message, lesson, or moral. This indicates that students would think strategically (level 3) at least, and if comparing multiple sources or texts, they would engage in extended thinking (level 4). Comparing the standard to DOK makes it clear that the standard is written at DOK levels 1 and 3, so the assessment should include the same levels of rigor.

Content Area: English Language Arts (Reading—Literature)			
Specific Standard: RL.2.2—Recount stories, including fables and folktales from diverse cultures, and determine their central message, lesson, or moral. Overarching Learning Target: I recount, or retell, folktales and fables, making sure to include the central message, lesson, or moral.			
Verbs or Actions	Receivers of the Actions	Additional Information (What, where, why, how, examples, teacher notes)	Detailed Learning Targets
Recount	Stories	Including fables from diverse cultures Including folktales from diverse cultures	I recount or retell fables and folktales from different cultures.
Determine	Central message, lesson, or moral		I determine the message, lesson, or moral from the fables and folktales I read.

Source for standard: NGA & CCSSO, 2010a.

FIGURE 3.8: Example unpacked document for Reading—Literature standard 2, grade 2.

If we were to compare the same standard to Bloom's, we would place *recount* at the remembering level, while *determine* would take students to the analyzing or evaluating level. Whether using DOK or Bloom's, we review the standard to build the assessment. This standard requires that students perform at both low and high levels of rigor to demonstrate understanding. Include both. The lower levels of rigor provide us with data that prove whether students remember what they have read. In order to successfully respond to the more rigorous questions, students need that foundational understanding.

ENSURING RIGOR

It likely doesn't matter whether you use DOK or Bloom's taxonomy to analyze the level of rigor, because both are excellent systems to achieve that end. However, you must use one or both of these tools to ensure that the level of rigor is not an afterthought but an integral part of the assessment-building process. The unpacked standard provides the information necessary to determine the types of tasks needed to assess students.

Let's look at another example of how to use Bloom's and DOK. Figure 3.9 unpacks Common Core Reading: Literature standard 1 for grade 4. The first part of this Key Ideas and Details standard asks students to explain the text and refer to details and examples when they do so. If we compared this action to Bloom's taxonomy, we would likely determine that students need to understand and analyze the text to find key information. Figure 3.3 (page 51) shared some verbs that we could consider to develop assessment questions or tasks with the appropriate rigor. The directions for such an assessment would inform students that they should answer all questions and support their responses by referring to specific examples and details in the text.

Content Area: English Language Arts (Reading—Literature)			
Specific Standard: RL.4.1—Refer to details and examples in a text when explaining what the text says explicitly and when drawing inferences from the text. **Overarching Learning Target:** When I explain a text and draw inferences from it, I refer to details and examples from the text.			
Verbs or Actions	**Receivers of the Actions**	**Additional Information** (What, where, why, how, examples, teacher notes)	**Detailed Learning Targets**
Refer	To details and To examples	When explaining the text When drawing inferences from the text	When I explain a text, I refer to details and examples from the text. When I infer from a text, I use details and examples I have read to support the inference.

Source for standard: NGA & CCSSO, 2010a.

FIGURE 3.9: Example unpacked document for Reading—Literature standard 1, grade 4.

Comparing the same part of the standard to DOK tells us that the standard requires questions or tasks at level 2 because students need to use their skills and understanding of concepts to provide details and examples that support their answers.

The second part of the standard asks students to draw inferences and support them with details and examples. On Bloom's, the rigor of this corresponds with analyzing and evaluating. DOK level 3 asks students to reason and think strategically. Whether you use Bloom's or DOK, the level of rigor is high, and the questions you ask of students should match that level of rigor.

Bloom's and DOK are not meant to bog down the assessment-creation process. These two tools can simply serve as reminders of the rigor associated with standards. The work you give to students should align with that rigor so that they can meet a standard's expectations. Without the appropriate rigor, students may do well on an assessment, but they may not actually master the standard.

You can build an assessment using the verbs and other language within the standard. This is an easy and effective way to design student work that is a direct match for the standard. Figure 3.10 (page 58) provides some generic questions that you could ask depending on the literature that students read. Notice that the directions align with the wording of the standard. Using this method to share the directions ensures that the assessment meets the requirements of the standard, and it gives students an indication of the exact expectations. Providing this information will lead to an increase in successful outcomes.

Part 1

Directions: Provide details and examples when answering the following questions.

Possible Question Starters

- Describe the personality of the main character.
- Where did the story mostly take place?
- Describe how one event in the story impacted the outcome.
- Describe one interaction between two characters in the story.
- How did the author get the reader interested in reading the story?

Part 2

Directions: Provide details and examples when making inferences as you answer the following questions.

Possible Question Starters

- What did the main character mean when they said, "_____"? [Add the quotation.]
   + What was the weather like during most of the story [assuming this has to be inferred]?
   + Would you be friends with the main character?
- Why did _____ [character name] _____ [action they took]?
   + How did the author provide hints as to the way the story would end?
   + How did the setting of the story affect the plot?

FIGURE 3.10: Sample directions and question starters for Reading—Literature standard 1, grade 4.

The questions in part 1 can apply to any piece of literature about which students provide details and examples. Students will need to give answers that are long enough to clearly explain the details and examples. In part 2 of the assessment, questions should cause the students to infer something that is not directly stated. The students will need to determine what they think is possible based on details and examples from the story. The key in both part 1 and part 2 is for students to provide details and examples that directly relate to their responses.

You may want to consider adding a variety of question types to your assessment. Fill-in-the-blank questions, for example, are very useful for recall of factual information. Figure 3.11 provides some examples of question formats. By reviewing the examples, you can see how the rigor or demand changes depending on how you write a question.

Question Format	Use	Example
Fill in the Blank	This format is typically used to report recall of information. Blanks of consistent length are preferable so students receive no clue as to the word or words that they should place in the blanks.	The main character's full name is _____.
Multiple Choice	Students choose the correct answer or answers from a series of responses. Teachers can increase the rigor of these questions by having students choose multiple correct answers or including the option "none of the above." When students select this last option, teachers can ask them to supply the correct response.	24 – 7= a. 23 b. 17 c. 31 d. 14
True or False	Students determine whether the statement is correct or incorrect. Teachers can increase the rigor of these questions by asking the students to make false statements true.	True or false: There are thirty-one days in the month of September.

Matching	Students match choices on the left with ones on the right. Teachers can increase the rigor of these questions by including multiple correct responses or having some choices on the right that will not be used. Students need to evaluate each response to see whether there is a corresponding choice.	Draw lines to match the categories on the left with the answers on the right. Types of quadrilaterals Types of triangles Square Right Obtuse Circle Rhombus Sphere Scalene Trapezoid Equilateral
Open Ended	Open-ended questions are free-response questions. Students determine the answer. Teachers pose the question, and students need to respond. The rigor can range from simple to complex depending on the task.	What motivated the main character's actions? How do you know that?

FIGURE 3.11: Question formats and ways to use them.

DESIGN THE ASSESSMENT

Assessment design can be flexible; teachers can cover all of the standard at once or break it down into parts as they teach the separate concepts. Teachers should also consider the type of content that students are learning. The mathematics standards include specific content. Expectations are directly tied to the mathematics concepts to be learned. However, the English language arts standards for reading for information, reading for literature, writing, and speaking and listening do not specify the content that teachers use. The content is up to the teacher, school, district, or state or province. For example, the Key Ideas and Details standard in figure 3.9 (page 57) clearly states the understanding that students are expected to demonstrate, but it does not mention specific literature to use. That is why I have split examples of assessment design into two sections: (1) examples of how to design English language arts assessments for the content of choice and (2) examples of how to design mathematics assessments for standards-defined content.

ENGLISH LANGUAGE ARTS EXAMPLES: CONTENT OF CHOICE

The fact that the English language arts content has not been identified gives teachers flexibility within and between classrooms. The materials that teachers use can vary to best meet the needs of the students, the grade level, the school, the district, and the community. It is important to know when choosing content and materials is an option and when content and materials are predetermined. If specific materials are to be used, they should be available to all classrooms. If there are school and district requirements, teachers should be well informed of them so there is no confusion. A balance between required and flexible is ideal. Balance leaves room for the pursuit of specific student and classroom interests. Required texts lay a foundation of commonality, which lends itself to collaboration among classrooms and schools. When teachers have common texts, they have the opportunity to compare and respond to student data, sharing ideas and strategies to promote student growth.

Another benefit of content choice is teachers can create generic assessments when content has not been identified. The word *generic*, in this case, indicates that teachers can repeatedly use the assessment to assess different content but the same standard. Figure 3.12 shares an unpacked standard in the area of reading. Figure 3.13 is an example assessment that can assess this standard with any piece of literature. Notice that the directions say students need to use specific details from the text within their responses. As a result, the assessment doesn't require a task or questions asking for specific details because details are already expected to appear in each answer the student provides. The expectation is embedded in the directions.

Content Area: English Language Arts (Reading—Literature)

Specific Standard: RL.5.3—Compare and contrast two or more characters, settings, or events in a story or drama, drawing on specific details in the text (e.g., how characters interact).

Overarching Learning Target: I use specific details from a text when I compare and contrast characters, settings, or events in the story.

Verbs or Actions	Receivers of the Actions	Additional Information (What, where, why, how, examples, teacher notes)	Detailed Learning Targets
Compare	Two or more characters, settings, or events	In a story or drama	I compare characters, settings, and events using specific details from the story or drama.
Draw	On specific details	To complete the comparisons	
Contrast	Two or more characters, settings, or events	In a story or drama	I contrast characters, settings, and events using specific details from the story or drama.
Draw	On specific details	To complete the contrasts	

Source for standard: NGA & CCSSO, 2010a.

FIGURE 3.12: Example unpacked document for Reading—Literature standard 3, grade 5.

Option 1
Directions: Use specific details from the text to complete the following tasks.
- Choose two main characters from the book you just finished. Compare the personalities, looks, and actions of the characters. Share how they are alike.
- Contrast the personalities, looks, and actions of the same two characters. Share how they are different.
- Choose two events from the book. Compare them to share how they are alike.
- Contrast the same two events.

Option 2
Directions: Complete the following tasks based on the two books assigned by the teacher. Use specific details from the text to write your responses.
- Compare the settings in the two books. Consider the geographic location, the climate, and the type of community (city, rural area, or other). Include any other aspects that are important to the books' settings.
- Contrast the settings in the two books based on the same considerations.

FIGURE 3.13: Example assessment for Reading—Literature standard 3, grade 5.

Review the tasks listed in figure 3.13. Consider what pieces of literature you currently use in the classroom. How might this assessment fit into your plans? Because the English language arts standards allow for flexibility of content, consider student interest when selecting content with which to teach the standards. Get student input as much as possible. Again, this depends on the amount of flexibility allowed in each classroom. If all content and materials are predetermined for each classroom, teachers must honor those requirements. If teachers have room for choice, options are plentiful. What would students like to read either individually or in groups? Decide whether there are books associated with what is being taught in other content areas. Allow students to select books for themselves or have input in selecting books for the class. This opportunity for input can increase interest in reading and commitment to learning; when students have a voice in decision making, they are more likely to take ownership of their learning (Michigan Virtual Learning Research Institute, 2020).

Now let's take a look at mathematics.

MATHEMATICS EXAMPLES: STANDARDS-DEFINED CONTENT

Mathematics standards already include content, so there is no need to determine it. Assessment design decisions are based on both the content and the expectations listed within the mathematics standards. While it is worth mentioning that assessment design allows for nearly unlimited format choices, we teachers should first concentrate on designing questions based on the expectation of the standard. The goal is to have the format fit the expectation. If the standard's rigor is at the evaluating level of Bloom's taxonomy, or DOK level 3, a matching exercise will likely not meet the level of rigor. However, if the standard asks that students know certain facts, matching will work well.

Consider formats such as short answer, fill in the blank, multiple choice, essay, demonstration, explanation, and so on. Combinations of any or all of these work well too and provide a varied format that can benefit students who relate to some methods over others. I suggest, as always, starting with the standard. Create tasks or questions that will evaluate student understanding of the standard; then determine the format. For example, instead of asking students the sum of 5 and 7, we could ask them to identify from a list all number sentences that have a sum of 12.

If a mathematics standard required students to recognize certain shapes, we would ask the students to choose all the quadrilaterals from a series of shapes that includes a square, a rectangle, a trapezoid, two triangles, a cube, and a pentagon. Other options would be to simply provide the names of the shapes and have the students draw them or to provide the shapes and have the students write each shape's name. We could also create a matching activity with a column of names and a column of shapes. The activity would ask students to match the name with the correct shape. Figure 3.14 (page 62) provides some examples of how teachers can design questions about similar concepts to correspond with Bloom's taxonomy's various levels of rigor, using either descending or ascending order of levels as preferred.

Figure 3.15 (page 62) unpacks a grade 4 Common Core Number and Operations in Base Ten standard. It asks that students read, write, and compare whole numbers. The specifics in the standard give guidance and details as to what an assessment based on this standard should include. Figure 3.16 (page 63) provides an example assessment based on the standard in figure 3.15. As with all the example assessments shared in this book, teachers can give it all at once or break it down into parts to cover each concept.

	Example 1: Number and Operations	Example 2: Reading for Information
Remembering	In the equation 2 + 3 = 5, 5 is the sum.	Where does the story mostly take place?
Understanding	In the equation 2 + 3 = 5, which number is the sum?	Why is the setting important to the story?
Applying	In the equation 2 + 3 = 8, which number is the sum? The answer is inaccurate. Determine the correct answer.	Describe how the setting is important to the story.
Analyzing	Jeremy said that 221 − 143 = 122. Explain the errors that Jeremy made. What is the correct answer?	If the setting were changed to a cold climate, how would the contents of the story need to change?
Evaluating	Show two different ways to solve the problem 25 × 68. Determine which is the best way to solve the problem. Explain why that way is best.	Provide specific examples of how the setting directly impacted the actions of the main characters. Explain your thoughts.
Creating	Create three different equations where there are three addends and the sum is 19.	Choose an alternate setting to the story. Rewrite a scene from the story, illustrating how actions would change as a result of the alternate setting.

FIGURE 3.14: Example questions at each level of Bloom's taxonomy.

Content Area: Mathematics (Number and Operations in Base Ten)			
Specific Standard: 4.NBT.A.2—Read and write multi-digit whole numbers using base-ten numerals, number names, and expanded form. Compare two multi-digit numbers based on meanings of the digits in each place, using >, =, and < symbols to record the results of comparisons. **Overarching Learning Target:** I accurately read, write, and expand multidigit whole numbers. I accurately use >, <, and = symbols to compare numbers.			
Verbs or Actions	**Receivers of the Actions**	**Additional Information** (What, where, why, how, examples, teacher notes)	**Detailed Learning Targets**
Read	Multidigit whole numbers Number names Expanded form	Using base-ten numerals, number names, and expanded form	I read multidigit whole numbers using base-ten numerals, number names, and expanded form accurately.
Write	Multidigit whole numbers Number names Expanded form	Using base-ten numerals, number names, and expanded form	I write multidigit whole numbers using base-ten numerals, number names, and expanded form accurately.
Compare	Two multidigit numbers	Using >, =, and <	I compare two multidigit numbers using >, =, and < symbols accurately.

Source for standard: NGA & CCSSO, 2010b.

FIGURE 3.15: Example unpacked document for Number and Operations in Base Ten standard 2, grade 4.

Write the word names for each of the following numbers.
4,768 _____
27,842 _____
19,005 _____
40,060 _____
342,073 _____

Write each of the following numbers using digits.
Seven thousand four hundred thirteen _____
Four hundred eight thousand seven _____
Thirty-six thousand sixteen _____

Which answer best represents the number four hundred seven thousand seven?
  a. 470,070
  b. 407,007
  c. 407,070
  d. 477,007
  e. 407,700
  f. 400,707

Use >, =, or < to accurately compare the two numbers. Place the correct symbol in the space provided.
12,329 _____ 12,239
4,020 _____ 3,978
48,999 _____ 48,889
70,070 _____ 70,070

Write the expanded form for the following numbers.
12,345 _____
45,003 _____
Seven hundred two thousand forty-five _____
Write the whole numbers associated with the following expanded forms.
4,000 + 300 + 40 + 7 _____
70,000 + 3,000 + 400 + 20 _____
In your own words, explain how you write a number in expanded form. Use the number 51,602 in your explanation.

FIGURE 3.16: Example assessment for Number and Operations in Base Ten standard 2, grade 4.

Notice that the assessment in figure 3.16 includes all components of the standard in figure 3.15 with one exception. The standard requires students to read, write, and compare numbers. A pencil-and-paper assessment can adequately assess the students' ability to write and compare. Reading numbers as well would require adding an oral component to the assessment. Students could do this portion of the assessment with the teacher in person, through the use of computer software or assessment tools, or through other means determined by the teacher.

Remember, again, that the format of the assessment is flexible. Questions can include multiple choice, matching, short answer, fill in the blank, or any other format that makes sense for the questions and the standard. Writing the questions first guarantees that the standard's expectations are met; then placing them into the desired formats will allow variety within the assessment. Format variety can help students perform at a higher level because they may relate better to some formats than to others.

IDENTIFY EXISTING ASSESSMENTS

When resources are plentiful and assessments are included within the resources, identifying the perfect assessment is always an option. In order to guarantee that the existing assessment is a direct match for the standard, comparison is necessary. Use the following steps to complete that comparison.

1. Review the unpacked standard.

2. Compare the verbs and expectations of the standard to the existing assessment.

3. Eliminate parts of the assessment that are not part of the standard. These parts could remain if you are using them to review previously taught or assessed items but not if you are using them to gain evidence of student expertise on the current standard.

4. Create tasks to cover parts of the standard that the assessment does not include, or identify the desired tasks within another assessment so the complete standard is assessed. Remember you do not need to assess all parts of the standard within the same assessment, but you should assess all parts at some point.

5. Check the rigor within the assessment. Look for the just-right fit. The existing assessment should be consistent with the rigor demanded in the standard. If you desire to add higher difficulty than the standard requires, take care to determine whether the student is proficient without the added difficulty. Student performance should specifically be based on grade-level standards.

Before reviewing existing assessments, consider whether designing an exact match for the standard would be more efficient. If not, locating an existing assessment is likely preferable. Many existing classroom resources, including textbooks and supplementary materials, label the standards being assessed. This is very helpful; however, you still need to compare the assessment with the unpacked standard to determine which parts of the standard are actually being assessed.

IN SUMMARY

Beginning with the unpacked standard is essential in all aspects of the teaching process. We rely on unpacked standards when creating a standards-based assessment. We rely on unpacked standards when making sure an existing assessment is standards based. Whether we are developing an assessment or using an existing resource, we compare the assessment with the unpacked standard. We review the assessment to guarantee it matches the standard.

Whether we create or identify the assessment, we ensure the assessment matches the standard's expected level of rigor. Using Bloom's (1954) taxonomy, Webb's (2002) Depth of Knowledge, or both helps achieve the desired match.

English language arts assessments are often generic, especially in reading, speaking, and listening. This means we need to determine the content that we will use to assess the standard. It is possible to repeatedly use the same assessment with different content to test students' levels of understanding. The mathematics standards define content, so in mathematics, we need to use the existing content to evaluate student understanding.

When designing an assessment, use the standard as the basis for creating or identifying the tasks to be completed. After you have created tasks and designed questions, you can set them in various desired formats. Use matching, fill in the blank, multiple choice, short answer, essay, and other methods of choice to provide variety within the assessment.

In the next chapter, we will consider how to determine the levels of performance quality on assessments by using rubrics.

Graphic Organizer Assessment for Reading an Informational Text

Read the informational text provided. Then complete the graphic organizer with the information you have learned.
List main idea 1.
List the key details that support main idea 1.
List main idea 2.
List the key details that support main idea 2.
List main idea 3.
List the key details that support main idea 3.
Use the main ideas and key details that you have listed to write a summary of the information.

CREATING STANDARDS-BASED RUBRICS

Rubrics give us teachers what we require in order to accurately understand what students know and can do. The standard provides us and our students with what needs to be learned, while the rubric defines the levels of performance quality, presenting students with clear performance expectations. Simply put, rubrics allow students to know in advance what *good* looks like. They are not taking their best guess; they receive a clear message written within the rubric descriptors.

According to the Center for Teaching Innovation (n.d.) at Cornell University, rubrics have a variety of excellent qualities. They make expectations clear to students. Not only do students know the important components of their assignment, but they also have a definition of quality to guide their performance. Rubrics also provide detailed feedback to the students based on their performance (Center for Teaching Innovation, n.d.). Rubrics allow students to understand an acceptable level of performance before beginning a task. Students can also use rubrics to self-evaluate their performance and review the higher levels of quality to improve their current status. Finally, rubrics support consistency of grading and take the guesswork out of scoring (Chowdhury, 2019). Teachers can use a single standards-based rubric for more than one assignment throughout the year. It is generic in nature, meaning that the contents are not tied to only one concept or one assignment.

In this chapter, we will look at rubric design, how you can introduce rubrics to students, and examples of standards-based rubrics in both English language arts and mathematics.

HOW TO DESIGN RUBRICS

To understand how to create a standards-based rubric, we'll start with an example. Figure 4.1 presents the unpacked document for a third-grade Common Core Writing standard. This standard in the domain of Text Types and Purposes deals with writing an informative text. Notice the first two columns of the document. These columns are the basis for our rubric categories. The first two columns of the unpacked standard state that students should introduce the topic. As a result, the first category of our rubric will be Introduce Topic. The goal is to keep the wording very similar to the unpacked standard; that way, students can easily see the connection between the rubric and the standard.

Content Area: English Language Arts (Writing)

Specific Standard: W.3.2—Write informative/explanatory texts to examine a topic and convey ideas and information clearly.
  a. Introduce a topic and group related information together; include illustrations when useful to aiding comprehension.
  b. Develop the topic with facts, definitions, and details.
  c. Use linking words and phrases (e.g., *also, another, and, more, but*) to connect ideas within categories of information.
  d. Provide a concluding statement or section.

Overarching Learning Target: I write informative texts to explain a topic and clearly share information.

Verbs or Actions	Receivers of the Actions	Additional Information (What, where, why, how, examples, teacher notes)	Detailed Learning Targets
Introduce	Topic		I introduce a topic, providing information about what is to come.
Group	Related information		I group related information to add to understanding.
Include	Illustrations	When they aid comprehension	I use illustrations when they help the reader understand what I'm saying.
Develop	Topic	With facts, with definitions, and with details	I develop the topic using facts, definitions, and details that help the reader understand the topic.
Use	Linking words and Phrases		I use linking words and phrases to connect my ideas.
Provide	Concluding statement or section		I provide a conclusion to give closure to what I have written.

Source for standard: NGA & CCSSO, 2010a.

FIGURE 4.1: Example unpacked document for Writing standard 2, grade 3.

We'll use three steps to create the rubric.

1. Define the rubric categories based on the first two columns of the unpacked standard.

2. Determine the point values or category headings for the rubric columns.

3. Write descriptors for each rubric category under each column.

Take a look at the example rubric in figure 4.2, starting with the first column. Notice that the column mirrors the first two columns of the unpacked standard document in figure 4.1. Next, look at the column headings. The headings can be point values or titles to reflect the level of the descriptors in the rows below each heading. For this example, I have included a number and a heading to illustrate both. Decide the direction of column headings. I consistently use the point values 1–4 going from left to right so students can easily see the progression of the descriptors; 1 indicates the lowest level of performance and 4 the highest. Some teachers prefer to start with the highest (most proficient) value on the left. Either way works, but please be consistent with whichever direction you choose so you do not confuse students. The point values provide a ranking system, but the descriptors within the rubric are central to student improvement. They give students specifics on how to achieve the next level of performance.

Standard Component	1: Beginning Writer	2: Apprentice Writer	3: Great Writer	4: Published Author
Introduce Topic	The introduction isn't apparent or doesn't introduce the topic.	The introduction attempts to set the stage for the topic but lacks clarity.	The introduction is clear and sets the stage for the topic.	The introduction is clear and interesting and sets the stage for the topic.
Group Related Information	Related information is scattered.	An attempt is made to group related information.	Related information is mostly grouped.	Related information is in clearly understandable groupings.
Include Illustrations	There is no illustration, or it is unrelated to the topic.	Illustration is related to the topic but doesn't enhance understanding.	Illustration assists with readers' understanding.	Illustration is very helpful to readers in understanding the topic.
Develop Topic	Limited or no attempt is made to use facts, definitions, or details.	Facts, definitions, or details are used to explain the topic.	Facts, definitions, and details are used to explain the topic.	Facts, definitions, and details are used to clearly explain the topic.
Use Linking Words	Linking words are not used.	Few linking words are used.	Some linking words are used to connect ideas and help in reader understanding.	Use of linking words clearly connects ideas and helps in reader understanding.
Provide Concluding Statement	There is no apparent concluding statement.	A concluding statement is present.	A concluding statement wraps up key ideas.	A clear, concise concluding statement wraps up the piece for readers.

FIGURE 4.2: Example rubric for Writing standard 2, grade 3.

The greatest benefits of rubrics are the information students receive regarding their own performance and the personal improvement decisions that they can make as a result. Rubric results can also provide evidence to support a grade. If that is a desired use, the rubric should measure student work that is summative, meaning students have had ample time to practice the standard being assessed.

When writing descriptors, be precise, and give students an accurate picture of the quality expected. I typically start by describing the highest level of quality in the last column and work backward from there. The highest expectation provides students with a goal to reach for. For the remaining descriptors, I reduce the expectation to best describe the attributed point value. The goal is to always have students work for the highest level of quality. However, when we evaluate student performances, all descriptors are available because the students do not always achieve the highest level.

Writing descriptors is about getting our brains on paper. If we know what we want students to achieve, and the standard gives us guidance, how do we best describe an acceptable student performance at the highest level of achievement? Let's consider the examples in figure 4.3. Compare the Simple Descriptors column with the Valuable Descriptors column. The major difference is that the valuable descriptor provides more detailed information for students about achieving the highest performance level. What does the highest level of quality look like at your grade level? Does wording within the standard help you describe the performance? What clarity do the students need to achieve your desired outcome?

Example Components of Standards	Simple Descriptors	Valuable Descriptors
Explanation of Process	Well explained, clear, and correct	The process is clearly explained and easily understood using complete sentences and correct academic vocabulary. The process will lead to a successful result.
Introduction	Captures readers' attention	The introduction captures readers' attention and sets the stage for the rest of the piece, causing the readers to be curious about what is to follow.
Conventions	Five or more errors	Errors are so plentiful they interfere with readers' understanding of the piece.
Topic	Clearly explained	Facts, definitions, and details are used to clearly explain the topic.

FIGURE 4.3: Examples of rubric descriptors.

Work from previous performances can help you write descriptors. Use it when developing a new rubric or tweaking one that already exists. Share the completed version with a trusted colleague for feedback.

Teachers should introduce the rubric before students begin their work—in the case of figure 4.2 (page 69), their writing. When introducing the rubric to students, provide examples for each level of performance. You can use previous student work for this purpose; this work does not need to come from the same assignment as long as the same rubric was used. To help students understand scoring using rubrics, distribute work samples to students, and have them talk through where they would score the pieces. Creating an understanding of quality work will increase the probability of quality outcomes for the students. Students are more likely to achieve what they understand. Rubrics provide a comprehensive group of descriptors to increase understanding (Ragupathi & Lee, 2020). Both teachers and students should continue to use the rubric while the students are writing to improve their performance's quality.

Scoring papers with a rubric is a matching game. The teacher determines where the piece of writing falls on each criterion of the rubric. Emotion doesn't enter into it; neither does effort. The object is to provide students with an accurate reflection of the quality of their work. Teachers can simply use a highlighter to mark each descriptor that best describes student work. The completed rubric is a source of feedback on students' work products. Students compare their results with the score the teacher marked for each rubric component. By comparing their level of achievement to the descriptors at higher levels, students can process how to improve. Certainly, the teacher can include additional comments and clarify as necessary, but the ultimate goal is to give students the ability to independently review, analyze, and improve their work. Students will initially need support and guidance before they become fluent at using rubrics to evaluate their performance.

Figure 4.4 features an example of student informative writing. Figure 4.5 is a completed rubric that scores the piece in figure 4.4. The shaded areas indicate where the student scored on the rubric. When students view a completed rubric, they can see where they scored and also review the surrounding descriptors to know the type of improvement needed to score at a higher level. The completed rubric also makes it easy to see areas of strength and areas of challenge to the student. The rubric is intended to not only be a scoring device but also provide valuable information teachers can use as a vehicle for student growth.

The Gambel's Quail
I'm going to tell you about the Gambel's quail.
It is a bird that mostly lives in Arizona. It lives in the desert. A desert is a hot area that gets little rain.
The quail eats leaves, seeds, and some cactus fruit. It usually lives over a year but can live up to four years. It likes to walk and run more than fly.
That is what I have to say about the Gambel's quail.

FIGURE 4.4: Example student informative writing piece for Writing standard 2, grade 3.

Standard Component	1: Beginning Writer	2: Apprentice Writer	3: Great Writer	4: Published Author
Introduce Topic	The introduction isn't apparent or doesn't introduce the topic.	The introduction attempts to set the stage for the topic but lacks clarity.	The introduction is clear and sets the stage for the topic.	The introduction is clear and interesting and sets the stage for the topic.
Group Related Information	Related information is scattered.	An attempt is made to group related information.	Related information is mostly grouped.	Related information is in clearly understandable groupings.
Include Illustrations	There is no illustration, or it is unrelated to the topic.	Illustration is related to the topic but doesn't enhance understanding.	Illustration assists with readers' understanding.	Illustration is very helpful to readers in understanding the topic.
Develop Topic	There is no attempt or a limited attempt to use facts, definitions, or details.	Facts, definitions, or details are used to explain the topic.	Facts, definitions, and details are used to explain the topic.	Facts, definitions, and details are used to clearly explain the topic.

FIGURE 4.5: Example completed rubric to score a student informative writing piece for Writing standard 2, grade 3.

continued ▶

Use Linking Words	Linking words are not used.	Few linking words are used.	Some linking words are used to connect ideas and help in reader understanding.	Use of linking words clearly connects ideas and helps in reader understanding.
Provide Concluding Statement	There is no apparent concluding statement.	A concluding statement is present.	A concluding statement wraps up key ideas.	A clear, concise concluding statement wraps up the piece for readers.

Review the student writing in figure 4.4 (page 71) and the completed rubric in figure 4.5 (page 71). These two figures are good discussion points if teachers are scoring papers written for common assessment purposes. Do you agree with the scoring? If not, how would you change it? Within teacher teams, it is important that members discuss and compare reliable data. We want to make sure that you and I would score the same paper very similarly. This means having *inter-rater reliability*, which refers to the ability to trust rubric scores regardless of who scored the task. We teacher team members talk through differences so that we collectively have a single mindset when scoring, resulting in our ability to compare results within and between classrooms. These discussions support the development of common expectations across classrooms. When first using a rubric as a team, you will find it useful to co-score papers in order to set common expectations and ensure inter-rater reliability. When scoring is reliable among all teachers on a team, team members can trust that results are comparable, and productive results discussions can occur. Teachers can brainstorm next steps, discuss student strengths, and work to eliminate challenges. More about inter-rater reliability can be found in chapter 5 (page 83).

HOW TO INTRODUCE RUBRICS TO STUDENTS

Take time to introduce any new rubrics to students. This typically requires only minutes, depending on the number of components. Share the components with students. Highlight the highest level of quality so they are aware of it and understand how to achieve it. You can accomplish this while explaining the assignment. If more time is available, you might want to share a completed task on a visual display and have the class score it with you. The amount of time necessary will vary depending on the comprehensiveness of the task. However, students will have a good understanding of all rubric components as a result. Positive performance outcomes are likely to occur when students understand not only the expectations of the standard but also the quality descriptors within the rubric. The following is an example of how to introduce a rubric to students. This example uses information from figures 4.4 and 4.5:

- -

Students, today, you will be writing to provide the reader with information about your chosen topic. We will be using a rubric to evaluate your writing. The Writing standard we have been working on shares that you will introduce the topic, group related information, use illustrations, develop the topic, use linking words, and provide a concluding statement. Notice that the rubric I have given you lists the same criteria in the left column. This is an additional reminder of what to include in your piece. Take a look at the column on the far right of the rubric. It shares the highest level of expectation for your writing. Let's look at each descriptor in this column. [Share that information with students.] When everyone is finished with their writing, I will match what you have written to the descriptors on the rubric and identify your level of performance. After completing the rubrics, I will share them with you so you can see where you performed. By viewing the descriptors, you will understand how your writing can improve and where you are right on target. The rubric and I will provide you with feedback that will help you analyze your writing. Before you begin your assignment, do you have any questions?

If you regularly use rubrics with students, a detailed explanation may not be necessary. If standards-based rubrics are new to students, a detailed explanation will help them understand the connection between what they are learning and how they are being evaluated. The combination of using the standard to guide their performance and using the rubric to view expectations will support high levels of achievement. In order to support optimal student performance, take time to introduce any new rubric before you use it.

Depending on your students and the grade level you teach, you may be accustomed to hearing a lot of questions as students get to work: "What am I supposed to do?" "Is this right?" "What should I do next?" "What do I need to include?" As often as is possible, respond to them, "Have you checked the rubric? Let's see if it answers your question." This way, students will understand that when they have a question, they should take a look at the rubric first. That will save their time and yours. It will also serve to make them increasingly independent as the year goes on.

Up to this point, we have only talked about introducing rubrics to students. You might not want to stop there. When parents know what a rubric is and how it is used, they gain a much better understanding of what their children are to learn. This gives them a much better understanding of what standards are and how they can impact student success. When parents know the expectations, they are much more capable of supporting your efforts and assisting students at home. You can share rubrics from kindergarten on up. I have used them all the way through middle school with parents.

Think about a fifth-grade student whose parents ask her if she has any homework tonight. She says she needs to write about a trip she'd like to take. This provides her parents with direction but little knowledge of specifics. Consider what the rubric adds to the discussion: It says the student needs to write an introduction. The ideas she presents should include facts, details, and examples. The body of her writing should state why she chose the destination. The writing should be logically organized so that the reader understands it. A conclusion should wrap up the piece. With this information, her parents have a much greater chance of giving her valuable feedback. I am not suggesting that parents are always available or able to help. Family situations and compositions can vastly differ. Yet, if any family members are able and available, rubrics can greatly assist them.

How do you make parents aware of the rubric and how to use it? Utilize whatever resources you have. Share an explanatory note similar to the preceding example. Post information and the rubric on your website. Add the information to your newsletter. Share it with those attending an open house, a parent night, or parent-teacher conferences. Provide students with an incentive for sharing it with a parent or family member. Mail it home if that would work best.

In my experience, it pleases parents to know there is a rubric. Rubrics clearly state expectations, which gives their children a better chance at success. Rubrics take the guesswork out of student performance and enhance understanding of learning standards. Give them a try!

ADDITIONAL EXAMPLES

The following sections supply a variety of examples of rubrics based on unpacked standards. We'll begin with some English language arts examples and then move on to mathematics.

ENGLISH LANGUAGE ARTS EXAMPLES: RUBRICS FOR PROCESS STANDARDS

Figure 4.6 highlights an unpacked kindergarten Speaking and Listening standard. This standard appears in the domain of Presentation of Knowledge and Ideas.

Content Area: English Language Arts (Speaking and Listening)

Specific Standard: SL.K.4—Describe familiar people, places, things, and events and, with prompting and support, provide additional detail.
Overarching Learning Target: I accurately describe people, places, things, and events.

Verbs or Actions	Receivers of the Actions	Additional Information (What, where, why, how, examples, teacher notes)	Detailed Learning Targets
Describe	Familiar people, Familiar places, Familiar things, and Familiar events		I accurately describe people who are familiar to me. I accurately describe places that are familiar to me. I accurately describe things that are familiar to me. I accurately describe events that are familiar to me.
Provide	Additional details	With prompting and support	I add additional details to my descriptions when my teacher prompts me to do so.

Source for standard: NGA & CCSSO, 2010a.

FIGURE 4.6: Example unpacked document for Speaking and Listening standard 4, kindergarten.

The standard in figure 4.6 asks that students describe people, places, things, and events that are familiar to them. This means that people, places, things, and events all need to be assessed; however, they don't all need to be assessed at the same time.

If you desire consistent assessment subjects, choose a person, a place, a thing, and an event that are familiar to all students. For example, the person might be the art teacher, the place might be the playground, the thing could be an object in the classroom, and the event could be a school assembly or celebration that has recently taken place. The uniformity created by having all students talk about the same subjects can be helpful in scoring the assessments. By giving all students the same task, you can ask students consistent follow-up questions and cause more accurate and comparable results.

Figure 4.7 is a rubric based on the standard in figure 4.6. In this version, the first column lists all components of the assessment. Under each component, prompting and support criteria are mentioned when the standard states them.

Standard Component	1	2	3	4
Describe Familiar People	One descriptive word is used to describe a person.	Two descriptive words are used to describe a person.	Three descriptive words are used to describe a person.	Three or more descriptive words are used to describe a person. The student speaks in complete sentences.
Provides additional details about the person with prompting and support	Provides one additional detail	Provides two or more additional details		
Describe Familiar Places	One descriptive word is used to describe a place.	Two descriptive words are used to describe a place.	Three descriptive words are used to describe a place.	Three or more descriptive words are used to describe a place. The student speaks in complete sentences.
Provides additional details about the place with prompting and support	Provides one additional detail	Provides two or more additional details		
Describe Familiar Things	One descriptive word is used to describe a thing.	Two descriptive words are used to describe a thing.	Three descriptive words are used to describe a thing.	Three or more descriptive words are used to describe a thing. The student speaks in complete sentences.
Provides additional details about the thing with prompting and support	Provides one additional detail	Provides two or more additional details		
Describe Familiar Events	One descriptive word is used to describe an event.	Two descriptive words are used to describe an event.	Three descriptive words are used to describe an event.	Three or more descriptive words are used to describe an event. The student speaks in complete sentences.
Provides additional details about the event with prompting and support	Provides one additional detail	Provides two or more additional details		

FIGURE 4.7: Example rubric for Speaking and Listening standard 4, kindergarten.

Notice in this example that when students receive support, the point value available is reduced. This is the case because the standard asks that students become increasingly independent. Students are aware that they should aim to achieve the highest point value; if a rubric uses descriptors instead of points, students need to understand that the descriptors increase in proficiency level. The goal is to learn and perform at the highest level possible to master the standard. When students are first learning and practicing the standard, they need feedback to increase their likelihood of future success.

Teachers can use rubrics as evidence to support a report card grade when the grade is based on summative work and students have had ample practice opportunities available to them. Rubrics are also valuable tools for showing growth in student performance when teachers have used the same rubric to measure performance over time. In any rubric, it is fine to reduce the number of point value levels for a criterion if multiple descriptors don't seem feasible. I've suggested that reduction for the rubric in figure 4.7 (page 75), but you can increase those shorter rows to a possible four points if you desire that.

Additional unpacked standards and corresponding rubrics appear in the following series of figures.

The task associated with standard SL.5.4 (figure 4.8) asks that students report on a topic or text or present an opinion. Because the word *or* is used, students can do one or the other; they don't need to do both. The rubric based on the unpacked standard in figure 4.8 can be found in figure 4.9. Compare the two figures to see how the rubric supports the standard and both provide information to support student performance.

Content Area: English Language Arts (Speaking and Listening)			
Specific Standard: SL.5.4—Report on a topic or text or present an opinion, sequencing ideas logically and using appropriate facts and relevant, descriptive details to support main ideas or themes; speak clearly at an understandable pace. **Overarching Learning Target:** I accurately report on a topic or text.			
Verbs or Actions	**Receivers of the Actions**	**Additional Information** (What, where, why, how, examples, teacher notes)	**Detailed Learning Targets**
Report *or* Present	On a topic or text *or* An opinion		I clearly report on a topic. I clearly state my opinion.
Sequence	Ideas	Logically	I sequence my ideas logically so my audience can understand them.
Use	Appropriate facts	To support the main idea or theme	I use appropriate facts to support my main idea.
Use	Descriptive details	To support the main idea or theme	I use descriptive details to support my main idea.
Speak	Clearly		I speak clearly so my audience can understand me.
Use	Understandable pace		I use a pace that helps my audience understand.

Source for standard: NGA & CCSSO, 2010a.

FIGURE 4.8: Example unpacked document for Speaking and Listening standard 4, grade 5.

Standard Component	1	2	3	4
Report on Topic *or* **Present Opinion**	Information is confusing or inaccurate.	Information is present but lacks clarity or is not stated in a complete sentence.	Information is accurate and stated in a complete sentence.	Information is accurate and clearly stated in a complete sentence.
Sequence Ideas	Ideas are out of sequence.	Ideas are accurately sequenced.	Detailed ideas are accurately sequenced.	Detailed ideas are accurately sequenced and clearly stated.
Use Facts	Facts are inaccurate.	Few facts are available, but they are accurate.	Ample detailed facts are accurate.	Ample detailed facts are accurate and clearly stated.
Use Details	Details are inaccurate.	Few details are available, but they are accurate.	Ample details are accurate.	Ample details are accurate and clearly stated.
Speak Clearly	The speech is difficult to understand.	The speech is clear.	The speech is clear with appropriate volume.	The speech is clear and expressive with appropriate volume.
Use Understandable Pace	The pace is difficult to understand.	The pace is sometimes understandable.	The pace is understandable.	The pace is understandable and varies according to the contents of the speech.

FIGURE 4.9: Example rubric for Speaking and Listening standard 4, grade 5.

Standards-based rubrics allow students to see expectations directly related to the standards. In addition, a scored rubric provides direct feedback to students. They can see not only where they perform but also the next levels of quality within the rubric descriptors, giving students a clear picture of what the highest level of achievement requires.

Review figures 4.10 and 4.11 (page 78) to again see the connections between an unpacked standard and a rubric.

Content Area: English Language Arts (Reading—Literature)			
Specific Standard: RL.3.3—Describe characters in a story (e.g., their traits, motivations, or feelings) and explain how their actions contribute to the sequence of events. **Overarching Learning Target:** I describe characters in a story, explaining how their actions contribute to the events in the story.			
Verbs or Actions	**Receivers of the Actions**	**Additional Information** (What, where, why, how, examples, teacher notes)	**Detailed Learning Targets**
Describe	Characters	In a story (for example, traits, motivations, or feelings)	I describe characters using things like their traits, motivations, and feelings.
Explain	Actions	As related to events	When I explain a character's actions, I relate them to the events of the story.

Source for standard: NGA & CCSSO, 2010a.

FIGURE 4.10: Example unpacked document for Reading—Literature standard 3, grade 3.

Standard Component	1	2	3	4
Describe Characters	Character description is limited or inaccurate.	The character is described.	The character is described accurately and in detail.	The character is described accurately and in detail, including traits, motivations, and/or feelings.
Explain Actions	Explanation of the character's actions is limited or inaccurate.	The character's actions are explained.	The character's actions are related to events.	The character's actions are described accurately and in detail and related to events.

FIGURE 4.11: Example rubric for Reading—Literature standard 3, grade 3.

Notice that the words used within the unpacked standard can assist teachers in writing the descriptors within the rubric. This is true of most standards. The first two columns of the unpacked document supply the rubric criteria for the unpacked standard; any additional information can be used to define quality expectations within the rubric. An example of this can be found in figure 4.11 under the four-point value. The Describe Characters descriptor includes the words "detail, including traits, motivations, and/or feelings." This wording comes directly from the unpacked standard, in the Additional Information column of figure 4.10 (page 77).

The first-grade Common Core Writing standard in figure 4.12 identifies the task of writing an opinion piece. The unpacked standard shares all expectations for students when writing an opinion piece. The teacher can identify the topic of that piece, or students may choose it, probably from a limited number of choices in order to narrow their focus.

Content Area: English Language Arts (Writing)

Specific Standard: W.1.1—Write opinion pieces in which they introduce the topic or name the book they are writing about, state an opinion, supply a reason for the opinion, and provide some sense of closure.
Overarching Learning Target: I write detailed and clear opinion pieces.

Verbs or Actions	Receivers of the Actions	Additional Information (What, where, why, how, examples, teacher notes)	Detailed Learning Targets
Introduce	Topic	Or name the book	I introduce a topic. I name a book.
State	Opinion		I state an opinion about my topic or book.
Supply	Reason	For the opinion	I supply a reason for the opinion I have given.
Provide	Closure		I provide a closing statement to my thoughts and opinion.

Source for standard: NGA & CCSSO, 2010a.

FIGURE 4.12: Example unpacked document for Writing standard 1, grade 1.

Notice again that the vocabulary of the standard is used within the learning targets. First-grade students might not be familiar with some of the vocabulary, but instead of simplifying these words, help the students understand the meaning of them. The vocabulary of standards often recurs, so understanding the words will help students as they progress during the year and throughout the grades.

The rubric criteria in figure 4.13 provide students with a step-by-step list of what they are to include when completing their writing. This is true of any rubric based on a standard for writing. The first two columns of the unpacked document give students the same type of information, but without the quality descriptors. Together, the criteria and descriptors tell students what they are to do and provide students with a way to understand how well they are doing it. When time is an issue or a rubric is not available, using the unpacked document with students is the next best option.

Standard Component	1	2	3	4
Introduce Topic or Name Book	The student states the topic or names the book inaccurately.	The student states the topic or names the book with minor error.	The student clearly and accurately states the topic or names the book.	The student clearly and accurately states the topic or names the book in a complete sentence.
State Opinion	The student does not provide an opinion based on the topic.	The student states an opinion.	The student states an opinion connected to the topic.	The student clearly states an opinion connected to the topic in a complete sentence.
Supply Reason	The student does not provide a reason that supports the opinion.	The student states a reason for the opinion.	The student states a reason that directly supports the opinion.	The student clearly states a reason that supports the opinion in a complete sentence.
Provide Closure	The student does not provide any apparent closure.	The student provides a closing statement.	The student provides a closing statement connected to the opinion.	The student provides a clear closing statement in a complete sentence.

FIGURE 4.13: Example rubric for Writing standard 1, grade 1.

MATHEMATICS EXAMPLES: RUBRICS FOR CONTENT

As stated previously, mathematics standards are content rich, unlike the process-filled English language arts standards. With process standards, rubrics are useful when attempting to define quality and measure levels of student understanding. Mathematics standards, although content driven, feature some student performance expectations that include important actions. Two key words that appear in several mathematics standards are (1) *explain* and (2) *solve*. The entire standard may not lend itself to evaluation by a rubric, but a rubric would be valuable to assist students in understanding expectations related to the words *explain* and *solve*.

The rubrics in figures 4.14 (page 80) and 4.15 (page 80) are designed to evaluate the portion of any mathematics standard that asks a student to explain or solve something. As a result, teachers can use these rubrics repeatedly.

Standard Component	1	2	3	4
Clarity	There is no written explanation, or it is not understandable.	The written explanation lacks clarity.	The written explanation is clear.	The written explanation is clear and in complete sentences.
Accuracy	The answer and explanation are inaccurate.	The answer is inaccurate, but the explanation of the process is accurate.	The answer is accurate, but the explanation is inaccurate.	The explanation and answer are accurate.
Process	The process used will not lead to an accurate answer.	The process used can lead to an accurate answer.	The process used can lead to an accurate answer. The solution is complete.	The process used can lead to an accurate answer. The solution is complete. The answer is obvious.

FIGURE 4.14: Example rubric for any mathematics standard asking students to *explain* their answer.

Standard Component	1	2	3	4
Process	The process will not lead to an accurate solution.	Some process steps are missing.	The process used will lead to an accurate solution.	The process used will lead to an accurate solution. All process steps are present.
Solution	No obvious solution is present.	The solution is inaccurate.	The solution is accurate.	The solution is accurate and includes any necessary labels.
Organization	Organization is lacking.	The organization can be followed with careful concentration.	The solution is well organized.	The solution is well organized, and the thought process is easy to follow due to the organization.

FIGURE 4.15: Example rubric for any mathematics standard asking students to *solve* a problem.

These rubrics include criteria that are important to successful completion of the performance, and they provide students with guidance toward achieving a solid response. The criteria become your choice when you base the rubric on a portion of a standard that gives no direction or definition as to the expectations of a quality response. In the case of figure 4.14, clarity, accuracy, and process are the chosen criteria for successfully explaining a response. However, you may find that different criteria are more appropriate for your classroom. In figure 4.15, the process, solution, and organization of a problem are deemed the important criteria. Review both figures, and consider how this type of rubric may be useful in your classroom. What other words in the standards may benefit from further definition and be supported by the use of a rubric?

IN SUMMARY

Standards-based rubrics are great tools to use to further define standards for both teachers and students. Starting with the unpacked standard allows us to easily identify the criteria required for an outcome that meets the standard's expectation. The format of the rubric allows students to visualize the necessary components that will lead them to a successful performance.

Because the English language arts standards are mostly process based, a standards-based rubric is ideal to guide and enhance student performance. Sharing a rubric with students before they engage in their assignment will support them in understanding not only the criteria that will lead to a successful outcome but also the quality required for an acceptable level of performance. Students should have the rubric available when completing their English language arts task.

The mathematics standards are content standards; what they ask of students is mostly clear. However, within the standards, students are often asked to perform a process, like *explain* or *solve*. When the vocabulary within a standard requires students to perform a process, a rubric is beneficial because it can list criteria that are important to successfully implementing the process. In this case, sharing a rubric with students will positively influence their work product.

In the next chapter, we'll take assessments to the next level by implementing common assessments.

CHAPTER 5

IMPLEMENTING COMMON ASSESSMENTS TO ENSURE COMPARABLE DATA

People make comparisons all the time, often without even being aware of it. We compare ourselves with others based on our height, weight, shoe size, looks, clothing, car, and dozens of other things. We want to know how we compare. It sometimes even affects our decision making. Consider how our comparisons would be different if we limited them to people living within our house. It would give us a partial picture of reality. It seems that it is difficult to know how we are doing without comparisons. When it comes to teaching, this is truer than ever.

When we educators limit comparisons to students within a single classroom, we also have a very limited view of reality. I know how my students are doing compared to each other, but I don't know how they are doing compared to students in other classrooms both within and outside my school. Are they achieving as much as others? More than others? Less? Comparisons help me recognize differences and similarities. They help me ask questions to improve my instruction and identify what I am doing that clearly helps students grow and thrive. Comparisons give us new perspectives. And common assessments give us a way to make those comparisons.

So what is a common assessment? A *common assessment* is an assessment used by one or more teachers for the purpose of reviewing data, sharing results, and discussing next steps for two or more groups of students. Common assessments are beneficial because they encourage teachers to increase collaboration, share new practices, and brainstorm ways to meet student needs. Discussing the assessment, its implementation, and the results can lead to positive changes in curricula. Through conversation, teams can identify effective teaching practices. Reviewing the assessment and the results leads teachers to discover new ways to improve the quality of assessments (Erkens, 2015).

Common assessments are extremely useful because they allow us teachers to compare how different groups of students did on the same assessment. When we have no one to compare our students to, it is difficult to truly understand how well they are doing. We know which students in our classroom are doing well and which need support, but would our top-performing students still be at the top if we compared their performance to the performance of the students across the hall? If students are struggling with a concept, is that struggle universal, or is it only in a single class? When students gain understanding of a difficult concept, is it because of the way their teacher taught it? Do students in other classrooms understand the concept as well? The answers to these questions help teacher teams determine whether and when the teaching methods have had a greater influence on student success in some classrooms or with some groups. Next steps can be easy to identify when we know exactly who needs additional support and which strategies may have the desired impact on student understanding.

The beauty of a common assessment is that we don't need to wonder. If the assessment is common, and implementation is common, the data will be comparable. We can analyze strengths and challenge areas. We can discuss next steps that we will take with our students. We can share teaching ideas and strategies that we will use to help students understand at a deeper level and enhance their performances. We can celebrate successes. And most important, through our collaboration, we can grow in our own expertise. The sections in this chapter will explore what it means for assessments to be common, how you can create and agree on common assessment practices, and how you can use common assessments in single-classroom grade levels. You will also find useful examples of common assessments.

WHAT *COMMON* MEANS

It takes time for a team to meet in order to develop common assessments. If the team uses the same process that we've discussed so far, this time is focused and well spent. Developing a common assessment does not take more time than developing an individual classroom assessment does, but common assessments do require more team time. When beginning this journey, determine the grade level's key standards. Identify an essential standard that is clearly important to student success this year and beyond. Because the assessment will be used across classrooms, this is a collaborative effort.

Collaboration time is sometimes built into master schedules. Some schools work on early release schedules, others have collaboration days built into the calendar, and still others schedule summer work. Teachers may even commit to meeting before or after school. No matter how you find your time, focus is the key. Prior to building a common assessment, take a look at the standards to determine which will be the basis for the common assessment. If you have not already unpacked the standards, be sure to do so, either individually or as a group. Determine beforehand what the team will accomplish together and what the members can divide up. The more work the team can do collaboratively, the more understanding and ownership the team members will have.

When it's time to actually develop the assessment, follow the recommended process in this book. Stay on task. As a group, determine what form the assessment will take. Will it be a question-and-answer assessment, or will it be task oriented, as with standards for writing that require a rubric? If a rubric is necessary, use the unpacked standard to design the rubric. If desired, have team members each take a rubric criterion and write the descriptors for that criterion. Then, team members share the descriptors, discuss them, and tweak them as necessary to agree on them.

To make the best headway, use time efficiently. Follow the process, and focus, focus, focus. Know what resource materials you will need available to build the assessment. If any advance preparation is necessary, decide who will do what by when so that when you are together as a team, you are ready to concentrate and make progress. Keep the following steps in mind as the team prepares for building a common assessment. Additional information about specific steps for common assessment implementation can be found later in this chapter (page 89).

1. Determine dates, times, and places to meet to complete all aspects of the agenda.

2. Decide in advance what resources will be necessary during each meeting.

3. Assign roles, such as who will take notes or type into documents at each meeting.

4. Complete an agenda for all common assessment creation and implementation steps.

    a. Decide on the standard to be used for common assessment.

    b. Unpack the standard if that has not already been accomplished.

    c. Create a standards-based rubric if needed for the assessment. (For example, a writing assessment needs a rubric.)

    d. Create the assessment questions and tasks.

    e. Write directions.

    f. Place the assessment in a student-ready format.

    g. Discuss and agree on common assessment implementation practices.

The process and products of developing common assessments are the same as those of developing classroom assessments; the difference is that teacher teams arrive at the process and products collaboratively. When developing a common assessment, we again begin with the unpacked standard. Figure 5.1 illustrates an unpacked standard in the domain of Text Types and Purposes for second-grade writing.

Content Area: English Language Arts (Writing)

Specific Standard: W.2.3—Write narratives in which they:
- Recount a well-elaborated event or short sequence of events,
- Include details to describe actions, thoughts, and feelings,
- Use temporal words to signal event order, and
- Provide a sense of closure.

Overarching Learning Target: I write detailed and accurate narratives.

Verbs or Actions	Receivers of the Actions	Additional Information (What, where, why, how, examples, teacher notes)	Detailed Learning Targets
Recount	Event or sequence of events		I recount (or retell) the events or sequence of events in a narrative.

FIGURE 5.1: Example unpacked document for Writing standard 3, grade 2.

continued ▶

Verbs or Actions	Receivers of the Actions	Additional Information (What, where, why, how, examples, teacher notes)	Detailed Learning Targets
Include	Details		When I recount an event, I include details.
Describe	Actions, Thoughts, and Feelings		I clearly describe actions when I recount an event. I clearly describe my thoughts when I recount an event. I clearly describe my feelings when I recount an event.
Use	Temporal words	To signal the order of events	I use words like *first*, *last*, and *next* to show the order of the events I am recounting.
Provide	Closure		I provide closure by giving an ending to the event I am recounting.

Source for standard: NGA & CCSSO, 2010a.

Next, figure 5.2 shares a standards-based writing rubric related to the same standard found in figure 5.1. The process we use is the same as in previous chapters. However, here, we have some additional considerations that come with developing a grade-level-specific rubric for a common assessment.

	1	2	3	4
Recount Event	The event retelling includes inaccuracies or missing components.	The event is accurately retold.	The event is completely and accurately retold.	The event is clearly, completely, and accurately retold.
Include Details	Details are confusing or missing.	One detail is included when describing the event.	Two to three details are included when describing the event.	Four or more details are included when describing the event.
Describe Actions, Thoughts, and Feelings	Descriptions are unclear or missing.	The event retelling includes a clear description of one of the following: actions, thoughts, or feelings.	The event retelling includes clear descriptions of two of the following: actions, thoughts, and feelings.	The event retelling includes clear descriptions of actions, thoughts, and feelings.
Use Temporal Words (Relating to Time or Order)	The student uses no temporal words.	The student uses one temporal word to clearly connect ideas.	The student uses two temporal words to clearly sequence ideas.	The student uses three or more temporal words to clearly sequence ideas.
Provide Closure	The retelling provides no sense of closure.	The retelling seems to provide closure but lacks clarity.	The retelling clearly brings closure to events by providing a concluding statement.	The retelling clearly brings closure to events by providing concluding statements.

FIGURE 5.2: Example rubric for Writing standard 3, grade 2.

Although figure 5.2 is a four-point rubric, we can reduce the number of point values in some cases. The key is to determine the number of levels of descriptors that you can successfully write. If only three levels of descriptors seem appropriate, create a three-point rubric, or if two levels seem right, create a two-point rubric. This is often the case in kindergarten and first grade; early grades have less sophisticated standards, so teams would not want to force extra levels of descriptors when they're not necessary. The descriptors should assist students in understanding the requirements of a quality product. The levels are created to assign a score to evaluate current performance and track future growth. The levels also help students understand next steps to increase their performance level. Keep the feedback factor in mind when determining rubric point values to ensure that the document has value and gives students a road map to higher performance levels. It's always worthwhile to discuss these considerations as a team to form a common perspective. Review figures 5.1 and 5.2 to again see the connection between the unpacked standard and the rubric. You can always adjust the rubric descriptors to meet your needs. Although it is beneficial to use the language of the standards as much as possible, the wording also needs to make sense to students.

The unpacked standard and rubric in figures 5.1 and 5.2 provide the starting point for building a writing assessment. The next step is to write a common assessment that multiple classrooms or schools will use to assess the second-grade students' writing expertise. Creating the assessment involves three important steps. Again, these steps are much the same as the steps of creating a classroom assessment, except the team members will come to consensus on all particulars.

1. Write clear directions for students.

2. Include the well-explained task that the students are to complete. Include all components that will give students the best chance at success.

3. If students have learned to read, provide them with the rubric. If students are not yet reading, orally remind them of the highest expected level of performance.

So does the team need to do everything together, or can team members divide these responsibilities? If you have the time, work together, as this provides the best opportunity for input and buy-in from all. If time is limited, do what makes sense. Everyone should have a role if work is divided so that all teachers have input on some aspect of common assessment construction. This is a learning experience for everyone on the team. Know that there will need to be some give-and-take. When team members work independently or in small groups, they share their products with the whole team prior to implementation. This way, all the team members can arrive at mutual understanding and acceptance before they identify the final product. One or more volunteers can put the assessment in a student-ready document if that doesn't get done during the collaborative team meeting. This usually just requires typing, formatting, or making the edits the team has agreed on.

After writing the assessment, write the directions. In the case of the second-grade writing assessment, you may give students a choice in what they write about because they might be inspired by one topic over another. Consider this point when developing the assessment: receiving too many choices can overwhelm students. Because this assessment is for second-grade students, two choices seem reasonable. While designing the assessment choices, ensure that what you are asking students to accomplish directly matches up with what the standard calls for. The second-grade standard for writing asks students to recount an event, so one choice might be an event that all students took part in. This choice guarantees that students have something familiar to write about. Students must be able to relate to the chosen topics. The goal is to see how well students can demonstrate the skills associated with the standard, so we teachers don't want the topic to confuse them or inhibit their ability to write. Figure 5.3 provides an example of a common assessment that includes choices for students.

> **Choice 1:** *Second-grade students, last week, we took a tour of our school and visited several areas. Your task is to recount (retell) the events of our tour in writing. Write in a way so that someone who was not with us can understand everything we did.*
> **Choice 2:** *Second-grade students, think back to last Saturday. Your task is to recount (retell) the things that you did throughout the day. Write in a way so that anyone can understand everything you did.*

FIGURE 5.3: Example common assessment for Writing standard 3, grade 2.

Students receive two choices in figure 5.3, and they should be able to write about either choice because both include their firsthand experiences. If we asked students to write about their favorite movie or the last fun experience they had, we might reach only those who have experienced or can accurately remember those times. Students all have different backgrounds and family situations. Some may have a plethora of opportunities and time for frills outside of school, and some may be working hard to care for basic family needs when they leave school. Being sensitive to students' individual needs and experiences will result in a common assessment that puts students on a level playing field, causing data to be more reliable and comparable. The goal is that all students have the ability to write about either prompt. Students who are not familiar with the contents of a prompt have no choice, and their ability to write will be limited. If you are interested in more information about recognizing potential bias and ensuring equity for your students, check out the book *Finding Your Blind Spots* (Nichols, 2022).

When writing assessment directions, ensure that the directions give students the information they need to be successful (and, as discussed, team members must agree on common terms and phrasing). The directions need to be presented in an easy-to-understand format. The vocabulary used should be familiar to students. The directions should use the vocabulary of the standards as much as possible, but the students should have familiarity with this vocabulary because the teacher used it throughout the lessons leading up to the assessment.

The assessment directions in figure 5.4 would appear on the same assessment document as figure 5.3. Notice in figure 5.4 that the criteria of the standard are in the directions. We want students to include all criteria within their writing. As a result, let's not leave the criteria up to chance. We can include them in the directions. We have already included them within the rubric. Doing both increases the chances of student success. If students still don't include all the criteria even when they are listed, the students likely don't understand the criteria, as opposed to just forgetting to include them. Not understanding calls for reteaching the standard, especially if it will not be taught again this year. If a student simply forgets to include a component, reteaching may be a waste of time since the student may understand how to perform successfully.

Today, you will be working on a writing assessment based on the writing standards we have been working on. Look at the choices listed on the assessment, and decide which one you would like to write about. As you write, keep in mind what the standard is asking, and do the following.
- Recount the event.
- Include details.
- Describe your actions, thoughts, and feelings.
- Use temporal words.
- Include a closing.

FIGURE 5.4: Example written directions for a common assessment on Writing standard 3, grade 2.

HOW TO CREATE AND AGREE ON COMMON ASSESSMENT PRACTICES

Now that we have an unpacked standard, a rubric, and an example assessment, we have the contents of a common assessment. But there are other things we must consider if we truly want the assessment to be common across classrooms. Unless also done commonly, these other aspects of assessment implementation can skew data, making it impossible to accurately compare the data.

Figure 5.5 lists various discussion questions that should be discussed as a team, school, or district before common assessment implementation takes place. Arriving at their answers as a team is the key to establishing common practices, and establishing common practices is absolutely essential. Once common practices are established, most can stay in place for the year. They don't need to be repeatedly discussed throughout the year unless changes are to be made or an assessment requires different types of responses to the questions. For example, with some common assessments, a team might agree that students will receive the time they need to complete the assessment. With other common assessments, a team might ask students to write a piece during an identified period of time so the team members see how the students can collect their thoughts and record them during a specific time frame. Review the questions in figure 5.5. Consider how you would respond to the questions; then discuss them with your team to reach consensus on the team's responses.

Dates and Time Frame	Will team members give the assessment on a common date, or will there be a span of dates? Will the assessment have a time limit, or will students receive extra time as needed? If students receive extra time, is there a length of time that the team should consider the limit?
Assessment Directions	Will team members offer directions orally and in writing? Are there directions on the assessment, and are there additional directions the teachers will give? If students ask questions about the directions, how much additional explanation will team members provide?

FIGURE 5.5: Questions to consider prior to implementing a common assessment. continued ▶

Supportive Tools	Can students use a dictionary? Can students use a textbook? Will some or all students have access to technology? Will a graphic organizer be available to some or all students? Will tools specific to the subject area be available for some or all students (for example, calculators, notes, or handouts)? Can team members read questions to some or all students? Will team members use certain methods to differentiate the assessment for specific students (for example, using a scribe, large print, or colored paper)?
Role of the Teacher During the Assessment	During the assessment, will all teachers on the team be actively observing students? Will teachers be watching for which students lose focus in order to return them to the task at hand? What guidance can teachers provide to any students who ask for assistance? What guidance can teachers provide to students who they observe doing things incorrectly?
Assessment Scoring	When using a rubric, will some or all of the assessment be team scored to gain inter-rater reliability? Who will correct or score the assessments, and in what time frame will they do so? What format will the assessment data be in so that the data are easy to interpret and compare? When will team members share the results with students, and in what format will they share them? Will teachers share results with parents? If so, when?
Actions Based on the Results	What result will indicate the need for reteaching? Are there concepts that don't require reteaching at this time? If a specific question's results are considered unacceptable, how will the team decide whether the question was at fault or the students didn't understand the content? Are there ways that the team can group students to efficiently reteach concepts as needed? Can teachers share students by grouping them across classrooms according to immediate needs? Does the team need to reassess one or more concepts tested on the common assessment?

*Visit **go.SolutionTree.com/assessment** for a free reproducible version of this figure.*

Each of these sets of questions—dates and time frame, assessment directions, supportive tools, role of the teacher during the assessment, assessment scoring, and actions based on the results—is vitally important. The following sections discuss the question sets in further detail.

DATES AND TIME FRAME

There are a few reasons to consider a common date or identify a narrow group of dates for a common assessment. The tighter the time line for issuing an assessment, the greater the likelihood that the assessment data will be comparable. If teachers give an assessment weeks apart, some students might have weeks' more experience with the assessed standard. The extra time could give those students an advantage, thereby making accurate comparisons questionable. For example, say that classrooms A and B are working on nonfiction writing. The teachers of both classrooms originally decide to give the assessment during the first week of March. But then the teacher in classroom B chooses to allow the students more time to learn and practice nonfiction writing and instead gives the assessment in the third week of March. Can this cause a difference in the results in classrooms A and B? I would suggest that there is a good chance the data will not be comparable.

Another reason for a tight time line has to do with students sharing assessment content. If one classroom assesses days before another classroom, students who have taken the assessment may have conversations about the assessment's contents or their performance on the assessment. Hearing these conversations could enhance the second class's performance. If this is a concern, tighten the time line.

Some students may require extra time when taking the assessment, and that is likely totally acceptable. However, teacher team members should make a common decision about that. If I give my students additional time and you don't give the same to yours because we didn't discuss it, my students may have an advantage that could skew the data. Answering the questions is not what's crucial; identifying the common practice is. The answers are up to the team.

ASSESSMENT DIRECTIONS

Assessment directions should give students a clear understanding of what they are to accomplish; they should provide any detail necessary to increase the probability of student success. It is difficult to know whether students will actually read the written directions. So it is beneficial to orally read the directions to students and provide written directions so that students can refer to them during the assessment. Discuss this among team members, and determine the preference.

Consider whether teachers need to give directions beyond what is written on the assessment, and be sure each teacher commits to providing the same information. For example, for the assessment in figure 5.3 (page 88), teachers can include additional directions if they have more to say to students. An example follows:

- -

Students, today, you will complete a writing assessment. This is called a common assessment because other students in your grade level are completing the same one. Teachers want to look at how students in the whole grade level are doing with their writing. We will look at the results, find strengths of all students, and maybe even identify some challenge areas that we will work on in the future.

You will have the entire class period to finish your writing. Please use your time for writing and reviewing your writing. As always, I am confident that you will do your best work. I will collect your writing at the end of the class period.

If you have questions while you are writing, raise your hand, and I will come to you. I will answer questions about the assessment but not about your writing. My goal is to see how capable you are without my input.

I will provide paper for you to complete the assignment. Now, let's read through the directions on the assessment together. We will also review the rubric that we have been using with our writing. It will be used to score your writing today.

[After going over the directions on the assessment, add the following.] Before you begin writing, do you have any questions about any of the directions or the writing you are being asked to do?

- -

The length and sophistication of the directions should match the age level of the students. The directions should be long enough to explain but not so long as to confuse. Consider your students, and respond as you and your team feel appropriate.

If there is a desire to provide students with extra time, team members should agree on a decision-making protocol to use across classrooms. This will ensure equitable situations for all students.

SUPPORTIVE TOOLS

Some students require supportive tools on a regular basis. These tools may include things like a calculator, a computer, a reader, enlarged print, and a scribe. Unless there is a reason to make an exception, students in every classroom should be granted use of the tools during the common assessment. Teachers should discuss and determine what supportive tools may be needed, who will have access to them, and under what conditions they will be able to use them. Consensus on what supportive tools to have available will result in equitable situations for all students and also ensure that data are not impacted by dissimilar practices across classrooms.

ROLE OF THE TEACHER DURING THE ASSESSMENT

The outcome of the discussion in this section is totally up to the team. Commit to a common set of practices. To ensure comparable data, your team must control for variables that can impact student outcomes, much as scientists control for variables to ensure good data in a science experiment. As a result, the agreed-on common practices become important commitments to the collaborative team and to the students. If your team determines that teachers will walk around during the assessment and pay attention to what students are accomplishing, that should happen in all classrooms. Consider how the results might be affected if I were the only teacher not walking around. Would some of my students be less focused? Could this impact their results? The point is that whatever you do, have it be common across classrooms.

ASSESSMENT SCORING

Come to agreement on how and when teachers will score the assessment. The *when* of assessment scoring means determining a deadline and identifying a date when teachers will discuss and compare results. The *how* mostly concerns assessments that teachers need to score using a rubric. Traditional assessments with answers that are either correct or incorrect can be scored without any concern about inter-rater reliability. Rubric scoring is different. We want to make sure that we are all interpreting the descriptors in the same way. When one teacher is scoring a student's writing, we want to be confident that if another teacher scored the same paper, it would result in similar scoring. Having every teacher score every assessment can be a major time commitment; this is not necessary unless the team prefers it.

Let's say we are a three-teacher team, and we have all given the same rubric-scored assessment. Then we each take the following steps.

1. Determine a date and time to meet.

2. Score two papers from your classroom to save time at the meeting.

3. Take the two papers, the scored rubrics, and four additional blank rubrics to the meeting.

4. Trade and score papers. Teacher 1 gives two assessments to teacher 2, who gives two assessments to teacher 3, who gives two assessments to teacher 1.

5. Trade again so all six papers are now scored by each teacher.

6. Compare the rubric results for each scored assessment one student at a time. If there is agreement, move on. If responses differ, talk through the differences until agreement can be reached.

7. Repeat this process with student assessments until you are confident that there is like-mindedness for each level of the rubric and scoring will be similar across classrooms.

At this point, teachers can score the remainder of their papers in their own time frame, making sure to meet the deadline established by the team so members can discuss the data. The data format should be predetermined so the members can make comparisons from identical formats. (Chapter 6, page 109, will discuss potential formats.) Identical formats save time and provide a valuable way to analyze student strengths and challenges.

ACTIONS BASED ON THE RESULTS

Before issuing the assessment and working with data, you may find it difficult to answer questions on this subject in much depth. It is possible to have discussions about which standards, or criteria within the standards, are essential and must be performed acceptably. Doing so will assist you in determining next steps when analyzing data.

If schedules allow it, have a team discussion about how it might be possible to share students during the reteaching process. Determining this will allow your team to group students according to similar needs. This is efficient because all teachers will be able to concentrate on certain concepts rather than having to deal with every identified need.

Acting on the results is the whole point of any assessment. What will we do about what we see? Data provide us with a direction that serves to improve student achievement. Understanding the data includes identifying strengths, challenges, and acceptable performances. As the team discusses next steps, review the decisions made based on the questions for acting on the results.

HOW TO USE COMMON ASSESSMENTS WITH SINGLE-CLASSROOM GRADE LEVELS

When a school has only one classroom for each grade level, teachers can reap the benefits of common assessment by using similar standards and identical assessments as part of a vertical team—that is, a team consisting of members who teach a range of grade levels. The vertical teams at an elementary school can consist of an early elementary team (including a kindergarten teacher, a grade 1 teacher, and a grade 2 teacher) and a later elementary team (including a grade 3 teacher, a grade 4 teacher, and a grade 5 teacher). Since it's very difficult to find time to be on multiple teams, one vertical team might share its common assessments with the next so that all teachers can take advantage of common assessments and get a sense of students' progression.

The Common Core English language arts standards, and other standards based on the Common Core, are written and formatted so that people can easily view the progression of the standards. They are also perfect to use for a common assessment that spans multiple grade levels. Take a look at figure 5.6 (page 94), and notice the similarities across grades 3–5. The portions in bold type, when compared across grade levels, illustrate the commonalities across the standards.

Grade 3	Grade 4	Grade 5
W.3.1: Write opinion pieces on topics or texts, supporting a point of view with reasons.	**W.4.1: Write opinion pieces on topics or texts, supporting a point of view with reasons** and information.	**W.5.1: Write opinion pieces on topics or texts, supporting a point of view with reasons** and information.
a. **Introduce the topic or text** they are writing about, **state an opinion**, and **create an organizational structure** that lists reasons. b. **Provide reasons** that support the opinion. c. Use **linking words and phrases** (e.g., *because, therefore, since, for example*) to connect opinion and reasons. d. **Provide a concluding statement or section.**	a. **Introduce a topic or text** clearly, **state an opinion**, and **create an organizational structure** in which related ideas are grouped to support the writer's purpose. b. **Provide reasons** that are supported by facts and details. c. **Link** opinion and reasons using **words and phrases** (e.g., *for instance, in order to, in addition*). d. **Provide a concluding statement or section** related to the opinion presented.	a. **Introduce a topic or text** clearly, state an opinion, and **create an organizational structure** in which ideas are logically grouped to support the writer's purpose. b. **Provide** logically ordered **reasons** that are supported by facts and details. c. **Link** opinion and reasons using **words, phrases,** and clauses (e.g., *consequently, specifically*). d. **Provide a concluding statement or section** related to the opinion presented.

Source for standard: NGA & CCSSO, 2010a.

FIGURE 5.6: Writing standard 1, grades 3–5.

Figure 5.7 highlights the similarities among these standards as well. It compares the unpacked standards in an abbreviated format. See also the blank reproducible version of this document (page 108), which a team can use for any standards.

Task listed in standard W.3.1: Write opinion pieces on topics or texts, supporting a point of view with reasons (and information in grades 4 and 5; W.4.1 and W.5.1).					
Grade 3		**Grade 4**		**Grade 5**	
Actions	**Receivers of the Actions**	**Actions**	**Receivers of the Actions**	**Actions**	**Receivers of the Actions**
Introduce	Topic	Introduce	Topic	Introduce	Topic
State	Opinion	State	Opinion	State	Opinion
Create	Structure	Create	Structure	Create	Structure
Provide	Reasons	Provide	Reasons	Provide	Reasons
Support	Opinion	Support	Opinion with facts and details	Support	Opinion with facts and details
Use	Linking words and Phrases	Link	Opinions and Reasons	Link	Opinions and Reasons
Provide	Conclusion	Provide	Conclusion	Provide	Conclusion

Source for standard: NGA & CCSSO, 2010a.

FIGURE 5.7: Example unpacked document for Writing standard 1, grades 3–5.

Next, a vertical team can design a rubric using the same criteria for all three grade levels. Variations in the descriptors will address the differences in the standards across the grade levels. Figure 5.8 contains a rubric that grades 3–5 teachers can use to score a common writing assessment based on the standards in figure 5.6. Notice that within the rubric, some descriptors are written in parentheses. The parentheses indicate that portion of the descriptor is connected to fourth- and fifth-grade standards but not third-grade ones. When used with third-grade students, the rubric wouldn't include the wording in parentheses. In fourth and fifth grades, the parentheses would be removed, but the wording would remain. This rubric shows all three grade levels at the same time in order to illustrate the similarities across them.

	1	2	3	4
Introduce Topic	The introduction is confusing or missing.	The topic introduction can be understood with careful concentration.	The topic is introduced.	The topic is clearly introduced.
State Opinion	The opinion is confusing or missing.	The opinion can be understood with careful concentration.	The opinion is clearly stated.	The opinion is clearly stated and directly related to the topic.
Create Structure	A structure is present.	An understandable structure is present.	A clear and understandable structure is present.	A clear and understandable structure is present, and it includes reasons for the opinion. (Ideas are grouped logically to support the opinion.)
Provide Reasons	The student provides one reason for the opinion.	The student provides two reasons for the opinion (that are supported by accurate facts and details).	The student provides three reasons for the opinion (that are supported by accurate facts and details).	The student provides four or more reasons for the opinion (that are supported by accurate facts and details).
Support Opinion	All reasons stated are clear.	All reasons stated are clear and related to the opinion.	All reasons stated are clear and directly related to the opinion.	All reasons stated are clear, and they are directly related to and support the opinion.
Use Linking Words or Phrases (Link Opinions and Reasons)	Linking words and phrases (or clauses) are not used.	A linking word or phrase (or clause) is used.	Linking words and/or phrases (and clauses) are used occasionally.	Linking words and/or phrases (and clauses) are used throughout to have ideas flow from one to the next.
Provide Conclusion	The conclusion is confusing or lacking.	The conclusion provides closure.	The conclusion provides a clear closure.	The conclusion provides a clear, supportive closure (that is, directly related to the opinion).

FIGURE 5.8: Example rubric for Writing standard 1, grades 3–5.

The vertical team's next step is to write the common assessment, keeping it as similar as possible across the grade levels so that results can be compared. The differences should be related only to the wording within the standards. The team should also write directions for students at this time. Figure 5.9 shows the common assessment and the directions. Parentheses are again used to show portions of the assessment that are to be included for only fourth- and fifth-grade students. Notice that in the directions, we teachers provide the expectations for students and relate those expectations to the standard. If we are expecting students to include all components of the standard, we don't want them to guess. When the expectations are clearly placed within the directions, no doubt surrounds them. We want students to achieve the highest level of performance, so the directions give them information to reach that end.

Directions: Students, today, you will work on a writing assessment based on the writing standards we have been working on. Look at the choices listed on the assessment, and decide which one you would like to write about. As you write, keep in mind what the standard is asking, and do the following.
1. Introduce your topic.
2. State your opinion.
3. Create a structure.
4. Provide reasons.
5. Support your opinion (with facts and details).
6. Use linking words (link opinions and reasons).
7. Provide a conclusion.

Choice 1: *Cell phones are considered useful tools. At what age should students be able to have their own cell phone? Write your opinion.*
Choice 2: *Some schools believe that students should be given homework on a regular basis. Some schools believe that no homework should be given. What do you think? Write your opinion.*

FIGURE 5.9: Example common assessment for Writing standard 1, grades 3–5.

After writing the assessment, the teacher team members review the questions in figure 5.5 (page 89) and proceed as they would if they were all teaching at the same grade level. The results will be comparable even though the students are in different grades. Areas of strength and challenge within and among grade levels can be identified. Plans for next steps can be created.

ADDITIONAL EXAMPLES

This section contains a variety of example assessments in both English language arts and mathematics. Any or all can be used as a common assessment. You will notice that some are in a traditional format, others are task related, and some are rubrics. Whether you are working individually or as a team, the process you use to develop the assessment remains the same. You start with the unpacked standard and use it to guide assessment development. There is a direct connection between the standard and the contents of the assessment. If they are going to use the assessment as a common assessment, teachers will follow the protocols listed earlier in this chapter. Prior to collaborating on assessments, team members may want to review the examples to support their thinking and discussion when developing their own.

ENGLISH LANGUAGE ARTS EXAMPLES

We begin with a Common Core Reading: Literature standard that asks grade 1 students to describe what they have read in a story (figure 5.10).

Content Area: English Language Arts (Reading—Literature)			
Specific Standard: RL.1.3—Describe characters, settings, and major events in a story, using key details.			
Verbs or Actions	Receivers of the Actions	Additional Information (What, where, why, how, examples, teacher notes)	Detailed Learning Targets
Describe	Characters, Settings, and Major events	In a story	I accurately describe characters in a story using key details. I accurately describe settings in a story using key details. I accurately describe major events in a story using key details.
Use	Key details		

Source for standard: NGA & CCSSO, 2010a.

FIGURE 5.10: Example unpacked document for Reading—Literature standard 3, grade 1.

The standard does not identify the story but clearly states what students should know and do with the information they have read. As a result, when developing the assessment, teachers will choose what students will read in order to evaluate their understanding of the standard. Since this is for a common assessment, the teachers on the first-grade team will discuss and identify the literature to be used across classrooms or schools when students complete the assessment.

Figure 5.10 sets an expectation that students will be able to describe characters, settings, and major events using key details in the story. This is a relatively short standard. We still unpack it because the list within the unpacked document creates a kind of checklist, where it is easy to see exactly what teachers have to assess. The document eliminates the need to go back and continuously reread the entire standard, thereby saving time and ensuring that all components of the standard are listed, understood, and included within assessments across classrooms.

Because of the nature of the standard, the assessment won't expect an exact answer as a mathematics assessment about money amounts, for example, might (see the next section, page 102). Answers can vary in most English language arts standards, so a rubric can guide students to a complete answer, which will help them accurately and fully demonstrate their understanding of the standard. For that reason, the examples in this sequence include the unpacked standard, a sample rubric associated with the standard, and a sample assessment. All three directly correspond to the unpacked document, again ensuring that the assessment measures what the standard asks, and teachers use the assessment data to judge how well the students can perform what is being asked of them. Teachers will compare these data across classrooms and use them to make decisions about whether to reteach, enhance, or move on.

The criteria listed in the rubric, figure 5.11 (page 98), are taken directly from the first two columns of figure 5.10. Teachers on the team collaborate on these descriptors to give students a clear picture of what a solid performance entails. The sample assessment in figure 5.12 (page 98) includes tasks that have students perform all parts of the standard. The assessment can be considered generic in that teachers can repeatedly use it with different stories. The content of the story doesn't matter. What matters is the student's ability to talk about the content—specifically, the characters, settings, and major events.

	1	2	3	4
Describe Characters With Key Details	Descriptions are confusing or inaccurate.	Descriptions of characters are accurate. One key detail is present.	Descriptions of characters are accurate and easy to understand. Two key details are present.	Descriptions of characters are accurate and easy to understand. Three or more key details are present.
Describe Settings With Key Details	Descriptions are confusing or inaccurate.	Descriptions of setting are accurate. One key detail is present.	Descriptions of setting are accurate and easy to understand. Two key details are present.	Descriptions of setting are accurate and easy to understand. Three or more key details are present.
Describe Major Events With Key Details	Descriptions are confusing or inaccurate.	Descriptions of major events are accurate. One key detail is present.	Descriptions of major events are accurate and easy to understand. Two key details are present.	Descriptions of major events are accurate and easy to understand. Three or more key details are present.

FIGURE 5.11: Example rubric for Reading—Literature standard 3, grade 1.

Directions: You will be writing about a story we just read. You will choose one of two stories. The goal is to write about the story so well that someone who has not read it would understand it. Let's look at the rubric together and go over the expectations.

Assessment: Choose one of the two stories we just read in class. [Name two choices for the students.] In your writing, please describe the following.
- The characters
- The settings
- The major events

Describe these parts of the story using key details that you have read. Write so that the reader understands the story as well as you do.

FIGURE 5.12: Example assessment for Reading—Literature standard 3, grade 1.

If the team wishes to do so, it can design a specific assessment to assess a specific story. Questions and tasks can vary, including multiple choice, fill in the blank, short answer, and more. Ultimately, the team should compare the assessment to the unpacked standard to check whether the specific assessment measures what the standard is asking. In this example, students are responsible for using key details from the story to respond to what is being asked. They are also responsible for describing the characters and settings.

If your team designs a specific assessment, review the assessment to make sure that it does not give the students the information they are required to know. For example, if we were designing a specific assessment about the story of "Goldilocks and the Three Bears," we could ask the students to describe Goldilocks, or we could list various characteristics and have the students choose which best describe Goldilocks. Choosing from a list still lets students show that they know which characteristics are accurate and which are not. However, if we were to state a description of Goldilocks and ask students to determine whether the description is true or false, we wouldn't know if the students could actually describe the character.

As with the example assessments prior to this point, you can use the preceding assessment in an individual classroom or discuss it with a team of teachers and make it a common assessment following the procedures suggested earlier in this chapter.

The Common Core English language arts standards include several standards dealing with speaking and listening. One of these is the subject of figure 5.13. Specifically, this standard asks grade 3 students to demonstrate their comprehension when something is orally read or presented to them. Students' ability to effectively listen and accurately determine main ideas and supporting details is being assessed.

Content Area: English Language Arts (Speaking and Listening)			
Specific Standard: SL.3.2—Determine the main ideas and supporting details of a text read aloud or information presented in diverse media and formats, including visually, quantitatively, and orally.			
Verbs or Actions	**Receivers of the Actions**	**Additional Information** (What, where, why, how, examples, teacher notes)	**Detailed Learning Targets**
Determine	Main ideas	Of a text read aloud, or of information in media formats	I accurately determine the main ideas of a text read aloud to me. I accurately determine the main ideas of media sources that I review.
Determine	Supporting details	Of a text read aloud, or of information in diverse media formats	I accurately determine supporting details for the main ideas of a text read aloud to me. I accurately determine supporting details for the main ideas of media sources that I review.

Source for standard: NGA & CCSSO, 2010a.

FIGURE 5.13: Example unpacked document for Speaking and Listening standard 2, grade 3.

The unpacked standard in figure 5.13 lists the details of the standard. Figure 5.14 (page 100) uses those details as criteria within the example rubric. Notice again that the pattern remains identical. The point is that this is a systematic approach—and since this is a common assessment, the third-grade teachers have collaborated on every step to make each component of their assessment common across classrooms. We do the same process with every standard. The result is a consistent, valuable resource that sets the stage for successful student outcomes. Students know because of the standard, the learning targets, and the rubric that they are expected to listen carefully in order to pinpoint the main ideas of what is presented to them. They also are aware that they need to determine the details that support the main ideas.

	1	2	3	4
Determine Main Ideas	The main ideas are not accurate.	The main ideas are accurate.	The main ideas are accurate and easy to understand.	All main ideas are listed, accurate, and easy to understand.
Determine Supporting Details	The details do not support the main ideas.	A detail accurately supports the main ideas.	Two or more details accurately support the main ideas listed.	Three or more details accurately support each main idea listed.

FIGURE 5.14: Example rubric for Speaking and Listening standard 2, grade 3.

Clarity is key. If we expect students to perform in a certain way, we make it clear to them. Students are more likely to achieve the expected outcome if they understand what it is they are required to accomplish. Share the unpacked standard. Share the learning targets. Share the rubric. Create directions that specifically state the expectations. And ensure that all teachers on the team are doing so. Ultimately, students will understand how the pieces fit. They will recognize in advance what they are to know and be able to do. When students know the expectations, achieving them is the next logical step. This process can't help but support students' ownership of their learning. Students will not have the misunderstanding that they are learning for the teacher; instead, they will understand that they are expected to master the standards and that they are responsible for showing what they know and can do. Providing a clear pathway to success will help students achieve that end.

Figure 5.15 highlights an example assessment. This is another generic assessment that can be used multiple times with different content—but again, for each assessment, teachers on the team agree on what that content will be. Notice that the directions suggest reviewing the rubric with students prior to completing the assessment. This is yet another reminder to students of performance expectations. If the assessment is used as a common assessment, all students should have the same opportunity to review the rubric, leveling the playing field for all classrooms or schools that are engaging in the same task.

Directions: Today, I am going to read to you a short story. [You could decide to read it twice.] Your job is to pay close attention to what is read. After hearing the story, you will write down the main ideas and the supporting details from the story. Let's look at the rubric together and go over the expectations before we begin.

Assessment: Students, now that you have heard the story, decide what the main ideas of the story are. Write down the main ideas and all the supporting details you heard as you listened to the story.

FIGURE 5.15: Example assessment for Speaking and Listening standard 2, grade 3.

The same pattern appears in the next example. Figure 5.16 features a grade 5 Common Core Writing standard specific to conducting research. This standard gives teachers and students an option. It asks that students recall information about their experiences or gather and then recall information about a topic. Figure 5.17 uses the unpacked standard as the basis for a rubric, which highlights student performance expectations. The example assessment found in figure 5.18 asks students to gather information rather than recall it. Because the standard gives the option, the team members can make that agreement when creating the assessment.

Content Area: English Language Arts (Writing)			
Specific Standard: W.5.8—Recall relevant information from experiences or gather relevant information from print and digital sources; summarize or paraphrase information in notes and finished work, and provide a list of sources.			
Verbs or Actions	Receivers of the Actions	Additional Information (What, where, why, how, examples, teacher notes)	Detailed Learning Targets
Recall	Relevant information	From experiences	I accurately recall information from experiences I have had.
Or gather	Relevant information	From print and digital sources	I accurately gather information from print resources. I accurately gather information from digital resources.
Summarize or paraphrase	Information	In notes In finished work	I accurately summarize (or paraphrase) information in notes. I accurately summarize (or paraphrase) information in finished work.
Provide	List	Of resources	I accurately provide lists of resources I use.

Source for standard: NGA & CCSSO, 2010a.

FIGURE 5.16: Example unpacked document for Writing standard 8, grade 5.

	1	2	3	4
Recall Relevant Information	Information is relevant.	Information is relevant and important to the event.	Information is thorough, relevant, and important to the event.	Information is thorough, relevant, important to the event, and easy to understand.
Summarize Information	The summary is easy to understand.	The summary is thorough and easy to understand.	The summary is thorough, easy to understand, and complete.	The summary is thorough, easy to understand, and complete.
Provide Resources	Resources are inaccurate or missing.	Resources are accurately provided.	Resources are complete and accurately provided.	Resources are complete, are accurately provided, and link to the summary.

FIGURE 5.17: Example rubric for Writing standard 8, grade 5.

Directions: We have been working on our research skills. Today, I am going to give you three sources of information. Your task is to review the information and write about it. Let's look at the rubric together and go over the expectations before you begin.
Assessment: In order to write about the topic, do the following. 1. Read the resources you were given. Determine the relevant information needed for someone to understand the topic. 2. In your own words, summarize the information provided to you. 3. List the resources at the end of your written work.

FIGURE 5.18: Example assessment for Writing standard 8, grade 5.

By now, the pattern is becoming clear. All as a collaborative process, the unpacked standard leads to learning targets, which lead to assessment specifics, which lead to rubric components. The consistency makes the process doable. The connectedness makes it logical. The outcome makes it useful to students as a road map to success and to teachers as a measure of learning and achievement. We'll follow the same pattern for mathematics.

MATHEMATICS EXAMPLES

Figure 5.19 illustrates an unpacked kindergarten standard. Review the standard prior to looking at the common assessment.

Content Area: Mathematics (Counting and Cardinality)

Specific Standard: K.CC.B.5—Count to answer "how many?" questions about as many as 20 things arranged in a line, a rectangular array, or a circle, or as many as 10 things in a scattered configuration; given a number from 1–20, count out that many objects.

Verbs or Actions	Receivers of the Actions	Additional Information (What, where, why, how, examples, teacher notes)	Detailed Learning Targets
Count	To answer	How many To 20 things	When I am given a number of objects, I count as many as 20 of them accurately.
Arrange	Objects in a line or a circle		I can accurately count objects up to 20 if they are in a line or a circle.
Count	Up to 10 things	That are scattered	When objects are scattered, I can accurately count up to 10.
Count	Objects	Up to 20	When given a number to count, I find the objects that represent that number.

Source for standard: NGA & CCSSO, 2010b.

FIGURE 5.19: Example unpacked document for Counting and Cardinality standard 5, kindergarten.

Notice that the assessment pictured in figure 5.20 mirrors the expectations of the kindergarten standard. Students have the opportunity to count up to twenty objects when objects are arranged in a line or circle. In addition, they are expected to count up to ten objects when objects are scattered. Students are then expected to count up to ten, and up to twenty, objects out of a group of objects. The teacher team came to consensus on all aspects of the unpacked document and assessment. The team members can verify that the assessment contents match the standard by comparing the first two columns of the unpacked standard to the tasks within the assessment.

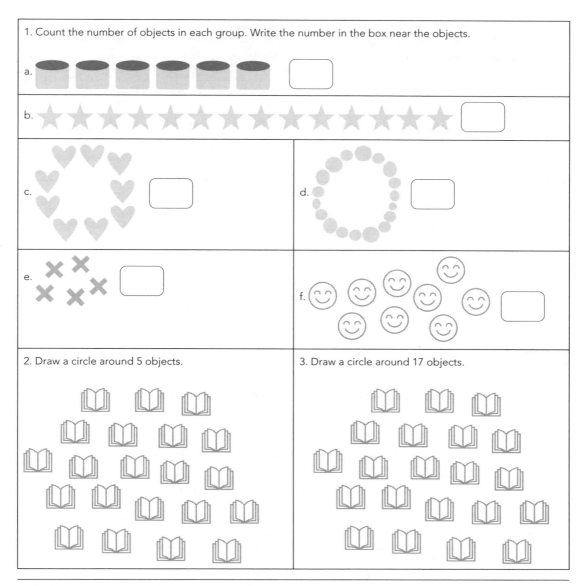

FIGURE 5.20: Example assessment for Counting and Cardinality standard 5, kindergarten.

Let's repeat the pattern once again. Figure 5.21 (page 104) shows the unpacked standard. As a team, teachers will build the assessment using the first two columns of the document to ensure that the assessment contains all the standard's components. For lengthy standards, splitting the assessment into smaller units is a totally acceptable practice. This standard does not need to be split. Notice that the third column contains no information for this standard. To keep the template uniform, the column is still included. Teams use the column as needed, which often depends on the depth of information within the standard.

Content Area: Mathematics (Measurement and Data)			
Specific Standard: 2.MD.C.8—Solve word problems involving dollar bills, quarters, dimes, nickels, and pennies, using $ and ¢ symbols appropriately.			
Verbs or Actions	Receivers of the Actions	Additional Information (What, where, why, how, examples, teacher notes)	Detailed Learning Targets
Solve	Word problems		I solve word problems that deal with money.
Involve	Dollars, Quarters, Dimes, Nickels, and Pennies		I am able to solve word problems that include dollars, quarters, dimes, nickels, and pennies.
Use	Dollar sign and Cent symbol		I use the dollar sign or the cent symbol when appropriate.

Source for standard: NGA & CCSSO, 2010b.

FIGURE 5.21: Example unpacked document for Measurement and Data standard 8, grade 2.

The assessment in figure 5.22 centers on solving word problems involving money. Word problems are the focus of the standard in figure 5.21 and therefore are the foundation of the assessment.

Directions: Solve the following mathematics problems. Choose and use the correct sign—either the dollar sign or the cent sign—in each answer. Place your answer below each problem.
1. While riding your bike, you see some money on the ground. There are 2 quarters, 3 dimes, 1 nickel, and 2 pennies. How much money have you found?   2. Ethan has 2 quarters, 1 dime, and 7 pennies. Janessa has 1 quarter, 3 dimes, 2 nickels, and 2 pennies. How much money does Ethan have? How much does Janessa have?   3. Darius opened his bank and found that he had 1 dollar, 7 quarters, 2 dimes, and 1 nickel. How much money does Darius have?   4. Lia earned 2 dollars, 5 dimes, 1 quarter, 2 nickels, and 5 pennies when she helped clean the house. How much money did Lia earn?

FIGURE 5.22: Example mathematics assessment for Measurement and Data standard 8, grade 2.

Notice the unpacked document clearly illustrates that the standard includes word problems featuring dollars, quarters, dimes, nickels, and pennies, so students are expected to be able to solve problems with all the money amounts. The brief assessment pictured in figure 5.22 includes all the components of the standard. The direct match between standard and assessment indicates that the assessment fully tests the standard. If the team wants, it can separate the standard into assessments that deal with one money amount at a time. At some point, though, students should be able to combine coins and dollars to solve word problems. Teachers can use figure 5.22 as an individual classroom assessment, or they may use it as the basis for discussion when generating a common assessment.

Next, let's take a look at a grade 4 Measurement and Data standard. Figure 5.23 shows the unpacked standard, which deals with area and perimeter. As with all examples shared so far, we start with the unpacked standard because it clearly states the expectation of what students must know and be able to do. Teams ensure that students have the required knowledge and skills before they assess. A direct match between the unpacked standard and the assessment assures all team members that, if the students perform acceptably, they have mastered the standard. The standard gives the team members detailed information on what to teach to help the students experience success. Individual teachers have freedom of choice and creativity in developing tasks and activities that support learning. When teachers compare their data, they may find that some practices yield better results than others and allow those who struggle to improve.

Content Area: Mathematics (Measurement and Data)

Specific Standard: 4.MD.A.3—Apply the area and perimeter formulas for rectangles in real-world and mathematical problems. *For example, find the width of a rectangular room given the area of the flooring and the length, by viewing the area formula as a multiplication equation with an unknown factor.*

Verbs or Actions	Receivers of the Actions	Additional Information (What, where, why, how, examples, teacher notes)	Detailed Learning Targets
Apply	Area formulas	In real-world problems In mathematical problems	I use area formulas to accurately solve real-world problems. I use area formulas to accurately solve mathematical problems.
Apply	Perimeter formulas	In real-world problems In mathematical problems	I use perimeter formulas to accurately solve real-world problems. I use perimeter formulas to accurately solve mathematical problems.

Source for standard: NGA & CCSSO, 2010b.

FIGURE 5.23: Example unpacked document for Measurement and Data standard 3, grade 4.

Notice that the standard in figure 5.23 asks students to identify area and perimeter in real-world and mathematical problems. The assessment in figure 5.24 (page 106) has students do exactly as the standard asks. If the team desires, it can include additional problems to make sure students can repeat the work correctly. Figure 5.24 is intended to show the full extent of the problem types required to meet the standard's listed components.

When teachers create the actual assessment for students, it helps to leave room so students can complete any work on the same page. This eliminates the possibility of errors due to transferring information from one place to another. Prior to implementing this assessment as a common assessment, teachers should discuss what they specifically want to see in a student's answer. For example, is work to be shown? Does the answer need to include a label? Is the formula to be listed?

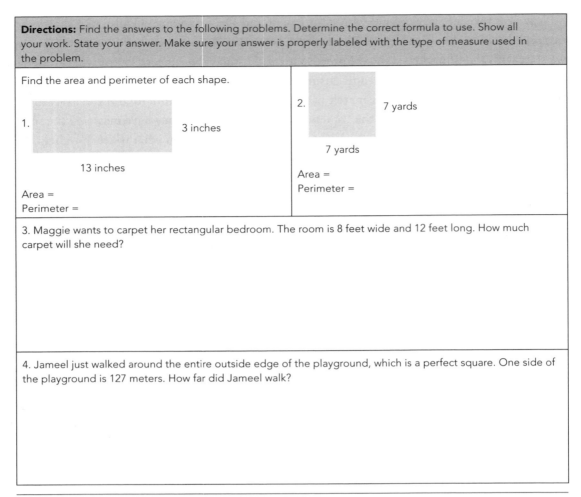

Directions: Find the answers to the following problems. Determine the correct formula to use. Show all your work. State your answer. Make sure your answer is properly labeled with the type of measure used in the problem.

Find the area and perimeter of each shape.

1. 3 inches / 13 inches

Area =
Perimeter =

2. 7 yards / 7 yards

Area =
Perimeter =

3. Maggie wants to carpet her rectangular bedroom. The room is 8 feet wide and 12 feet long. How much carpet will she need?

4. Jameel just walked around the entire outside edge of the playground, which is a perfect square. One side of the playground is 127 meters. How far did Jameel walk?

FIGURE 5.24: Example assessment for Measurement and Data standard 3, grade 4.

The preceding examples are intended to demonstrate the pattern and show connections among the standards, the unpacked documents, the learning targets, the rubrics, and the assessments. Students will understand these items as a complete unit rather than isolated items that have unclear connections. These pieces are not unique events. They are connected and create stepping-stones to student achievement. The entire package provides the information students need in order to perform successfully and understand how what they are learning is connected. Their learning is part of a master plan, a bigger picture. They are not learning a skill for the day but engaging in a connected group of activities and assessments that lead to the global outcomes stated in the standards. The fact that teacher teams collaborate on implementing the standards also ensures students consistently receive these messages and see learning as something purposeful that impacts them not just today but for a lifetime.

IN SUMMARY

This chapter provided clarity and connections for a continuous process. Common assessments are directly linked to the work illustrated in all previous chapters. As with all other steps, the starting point of implementing common assessments is the unpacked standard.

Building common assessments is a collaborative effort. Although the process remains the same as when designing a classroom assessment, teachers work together to determine how they will assess the standard. They might design the actual assessment or identify it within existing materials.

Prior to using the common assessment, teachers must have discussions regarding consistency of implementation; these discussions are crucial to gathering comparable data. Figure 5.5 (page 89) lists several points that teacher team members should talk about before giving the common assessment so they reach agreement on all aspects of implementation.

When a school has only one classroom of each grade level, making exact comparisons is unlikely. Comparisons are possible, though, when a vertical team of teachers uses standards that build from one year to the next, like those for English language arts. The teachers can compare the assessments because the standards are similar. The discussions and collaboration that follow the common assessments are worth the effort it takes to build similar common assessments at different grade levels. Single-classroom grade levels should not be deterrents to common assessment implementation.

The examples included in this chapter encourage standards-based assessment selection and design. Standards-aligned assessments serve to provide quality, actionable data, which is the subject of the next chapter.

Unpacked Standards Document for Vertical Teams

Task listed in standard:					
Grade		Grade		Grade	
Actions	Receivers of the Actions	Actions	Receivers of the Actions	Actions	Receivers of the Actions

CHAPTER 6

USING UNPACKED STANDARDS TO REPORT DATA AND CREATE A SCOPE AND SEQUENCE

If you are anything like me, looking at the data from an assessment you gave might have caused you to say to yourself, "Now what do I do? What do I reteach? Are there errors that I can ignore and the students will be OK? How do I manage all that the data tell me? How do I relate the test items to what I have taught?"

Data can be overwhelming! They certainly were for me, at least until I began to link the assessment to the standard and the data to the assessment. These connections create a clear pathway that indicates where the errors lie. They directly associate the pieces of the unpacked standard with what is taught and how it is tested, making it possible to prepare for an assessment's outcome before the assessment is administered.

Using data to monitor student progress leads to improved student achievement (Timperley, 2009). Teachers can make relevant adjustments to classroom practices in order to meet student needs. They can evaluate practices to gauge the practices' impact on student understanding. Conversations with colleagues serve to expand teaching practices when teachers are planning to respond to data. Monitoring data is essential.

Certainly, having data isn't enough. We teachers need to use the data. Being curious about data is a good step toward that. What are the data telling us? What, if anything, do we want to do about them? How can we support each other when responding to our data (Lipton & Wellman, 2012)?

Before getting into the chapter, I would like to acknowledge something that, by now, may seem like it's missing. Throughout this book, I have concentrated on using standards as the basis for teaching and assessment. I have not connected this work to grading practices; my primary focus is to give you a process for standards and assessment that works. However, if you would like to know more about grading in a standards-based system, I highly recommend Tom Schimmer's (2016a) book *Grading From the Inside Out: Bringing Accuracy to Student Assessment Through a Standards-Based Mindset*.

In this chapter, we will explore two different topics. First, we'll take a look at standards-based data reports and how to act on them. As in previous chapters, the starting point will be unpacking the standard. Next, again using the unpacked standard, we'll create a document that can illuminate the scope and sequence of the standards-based process. In both cases, this chapter shares examples featuring Common Core English language arts and mathematics standards.

HOW TO ACT ON DATA REPORTS

When reporting data, teachers benefit from a format that is easy to interpret. The less time it takes to understand the way data are being presented, the more time teachers can spend evaluating preferred next steps. Using a standards-based approach ties the pieces together in a connected, actionable package.

As an individual or a team, determine what helps you understand data. Do you or any members of your team love statistics and like to manipulate data? Perhaps you want to consider using a spreadsheet program such as Microsoft Excel or some type of data warehouse. If you are looking for something less sophisticated, consider color-coded charts. If you already have a data-reporting method that works for you or your team, keep using it. Just incorporate the standards into the current format. The following sections, divided into rubric-scored and non-rubric-scored examples, will give you some ideas about how to make data-formatting decisions.

ENGLISH LANGUAGE ARTS EXAMPLES: RUBRIC SCORED

As always, we start with the unpacked standard. Here, let's begin with the unpacked grade 5 Common Core Writing standard in figure 6.1. Notice that, as in all other examples, the unpacked standard columns clearly tell the students what they are to do. The Detailed Learning Targets column shares why the unpacked pieces are necessary and helps students understand what is expected of them.

Content Area: English Language Arts (Writing)

Specific Standard: W.5.3—Write narratives to develop real or imagined experiences or events using effective technique, descriptive details, and clear event sequences.
   a. Orient the reader by establishing a situation and introducing a narrator and/or characters; organize an event sequence that unfolds naturally.
   b. Use narrative techniques, such as dialogue, description, and pacing, to develop experiences and events or show the responses of characters to situations.
   c. Use a variety of transitional words, phrases, and clauses to manage the sequence of events.
   d. Use concrete words and phrases and sensory details to convey experiences and events precisely.
   e. Provide a conclusion that follows from the narrated experiences or events.

Overarching Learning Target: I effectively write narratives that develop experiences and events.

Verbs or Actions	Receivers of the Actions	Additional Information (What, where, why, how, examples, teacher notes)	Detailed Learning Targets
Orient	Reader	By establishing the situation	I help the reader understand what I will be writing about by establishing the situation.
Introduce	Narrator or characters		I introduce the characters so the reader gets to know them.
Organize	Event sequence	That unfolds naturally	I organize events in a sequence that helps the reader understand my story.
Use	Narrative techniques	Like dialogue, description, and pacing to develop experiences and events	I use different techniques to develop and add interest to my writing.
Use	Transitional words, Phrases, and Clauses	To sequence events	I use transitions so that my writing flows from one event to the next.
Use	Concrete words and phrases and Sensory words	To convey experiences and events	I include words that enhance the experience of the reader by creating feelings and pictures that add interest to the story.
Provide	Conclusion	That follows from experiences and events	I include a conclusion that follows from experiences and events and wraps up my writing.

Source for standard: NGA & CCSSO, 2010a.

FIGURE 6.1: Unpacked document for Writing standard 3, grade 5.

As in the previous chapter, the rubric in figure 6.2 (page 112) uses the first two columns of the unpacked document as criteria. These criteria will lead to a successful performance if well implemented. The rubric descriptors share expectations of a quality performance. Notice that some of the level 4 descriptors include wording directly from the standard because the standard has a clear expectation of quality. One such example is the level 4 descriptor for the Use Transitions criterion, which uses words taken directly from the standard's specifications.

When we have the unpacked standard and are evaluating student performance with a rubric, the rubric criteria form the basis of data collection. These criteria automatically match the standard, the unpacked document, and the learning targets, and the rubric helps us gather data associated with student strengths and challenges specific to the rubric criteria.

Figure 6.3 (page 113) features an example data display for the results of an assessment scored with the rubric in figure 6.2. For the sake of space, this example data display shows results for only six students. The display will work the same with as many students as you have.

	1	2	3	4
Orient Reader	No effective attempt is made to prepare the reader for what is to follow.	An attempt is made to orient the reader to what is to follow.	The reader is successfully oriented to what is to follow.	The writer successfully and dynamically acquaints the reader with what is to follow.
Introduce Characters	Little or no information is shared as characters are introduced.	Some information is shared as characters are introduced.	The reader understands who the characters are as a result of the introduction.	Characters come to life as they are introduced, giving the reader a clear understanding of who the characters are and what they are like.
Organize Sequence	The sequence is distracting or confusing.	The organization is apparent but can be confusing.	The organization adds clarity to the piece.	The sequence of events adds interest and clarity for the reader.
Use Narrative Techniques	There is no apparent use of narrative techniques.	An attempt is made to use a narrative technique.	Two narrative techniques are used effectively.	Narrative techniques, including dialogue, description, and pacing, are appropriately used to develop experiences and events.
Use Transitions	Transitions are not used.	A few transitions are used to help with the flow of the piece.	Several transitions are used to help with the flow of the piece.	Transitional words, phrases, and clauses are used effectively to create a smooth flow in the piece.
Use Words	Few descriptive words are used.	Limited descriptions are used, providing some words, phrases, or sensory words.	Many descriptions are used, providing some words, phrases, or sensory words.	Concrete words, phrases, and sensory words are used throughout the piece.
Provide Conclusion	A conclusion is confusing or missing.	A conclusion is attempted with no sense of closure.	A basic conclusion is present and provides a clear ending to the piece.	The conclusion adds a complete and effective sense of closure to the piece.

FIGURE 6.2: Example rubric for Writing standard 3, grade 5.

	Orient Reader	Introduce Characters	Organize Sequence	Use Narrative Techniques	Use Transitions	Use Words	Provide Conclusion	Mode
Student 1	3	3	4	4	3	3	4	1s = 0 2s = 0 3s = 4 4s = 3 Mode = 3
Student 2	2	3	4	4	4	3	4	1s = 0 2s = 1 3s = 2 4s = 4 Mode = 4
Student 3	2	4	3	4	3	4	4	1s = 0 2s = 1 3s = 2 4s = 4 Mode = 4
Student 4	3	3	4	4	2	3	3	1s = 0 2s = 1 3s = 4 4s = 2 Mode = 3
Student 5	3	4	4	4	3	3	4	1s = 0 2s = 0 3s = 3 4s = 4 Mode = 4
Student 6	2	4	3	4	3	4	4	1s = 0 2s = 1 3s = 2 4s = 4 Mode = 4
Number of Students Receiving Each Score	1s = 0 2s = 3 3s = 3 4s = 0 Modes = 2 and 3	1s = 0 2s = 0 3s = 3 4s = 3 Modes = 3 and 4	1s = 0 2s = 0 3s = 2 4s = 4 Mode = 4	1s = 0 2s = 0 3s = 0 4s = 6 Mode = 4	1s = 0 2s = 1 3s = 4 4s = 1 Mode = 3	1s = 0 2s = 0 3s = 4 4s = 2 Mode = 3	1s = 0 2s = 0 3s = 1 4s = 5 Mode = 4	

FIGURE 6.3: Example data display for Writing standard 3, grade 5.

How you collect and report the data is dependent on the tools available to you. If you use a computer-based data collection and reporting tool, determine how you can place the needed information into the tool for analysis. In this case, you need to report on the rubric criteria individually so you can determine action steps. If you are comfortable using spreadsheets, you can place the information into a spreadsheet and analyze it with that tool. If you prefer paper and pencil, you can use a class list to record the data. This recording method can fit into whatever system you use to collect and report on data.

Now let's talk about the contents of the display. Notice that the criteria from the rubric are listed across the top of the data display. The first column includes student names, and the last column shows score totals and the mode of the rubric results. You will recall that the *mode* is the number that appears most often in a data set. Averaging can be misleading and limit the information provided. For example, let's say a student received the scores 4, 4, 4, and 1. The average of these four scores is 3.25, which indicates that the student is doing well, but not stellar. It doesn't give us the actionable information supplied by all four scores. The student received the top score in three areas but has a significant need in one area. An average can mask needs as well as strengths. However, looking at both mode and average can give us different perspectives on the same data, and comparing the two provides a potentially interesting picture. The last column of the chart indicates how many of each score the student received, with the final statement identifying the mode for that student. The final row of the data display indicates how many students earned each score listed in the column.

The data in figure 6.3 (page 113) include only numbers. If possible for you, I suggest color-coding the data. I usually use blue for 4s, green for 3s, yellow for 2s, and red for 1s. Color coding makes the numbers stand out, thereby supporting teachers' ability to analyze the data fairly quickly.

Before moving on, familiarize yourself with the data in figure 6.3. Let's consider what you might want to learn from the information presented in figure 6.3. Figure 6.4 includes some basic questions to spur thought.

Questions about whole-group results
1. On what criteria (items) did the students perform well? Why?
2. On what criteria did students struggle? Why?
3. Are there any noticeable patterns in the data? What are they?
4. Are there areas that need to be retaught to the whole class? When?
5. Are there noticeable errors or mistakes?
6. Are there teaching methods that worked particularly well?

Questions about individual and subgroup results
7. Which students need support on which criteria?
8. Are there students with common needs? Can I group them to reteach concepts?
9. Did students perform differently depending on their gender? How about depending on other subgroupings (for example, ethnicity, special education status, or socioeconomic status)? Why might that be the case? What will I do about it?
10. Is there anything else I wonder about these results?

FIGURE 6.4: Sample questions to consider during data analysis.

Visit go.SolutionTree.com/assessment for a free reproducible version of this figure.

Start with basic questions, but go where the data take you. Often, the data will cause other questions to surface. Consider additional questions that you would like to pose as you review your data. You will notice that we review whole-group and individual results. This creates a comparison and provides a better indication as to how a student is performing. Ideally, we compare students to themselves and to their peers in order to get a well-rounded picture of student performance. In addition, consider students who consistently perform well and are at or near the top of their class. We want to make sure that high-performing students continue to improve and grow, which is why we compare them to themselves. The goal with common assessments is to compare student to class and class to class. The comparison provides us with information that helps us better understand student performance from a variety of viewpoints.

Next, we'll use questions listed in figure 6.4 to analyze the data in figure 6.3. Because the data are based on a four-point rubric, we will assume that 3s and 4s are acceptable scores, as is typical with a four-point rubric; these scores usually represent proficiency and mastery, respectively.

Whole-group performance indicates that all students performed well on five of the seven criteria. All students received a 4 when scored on Use Narrative Techniques. With results like this, it would be beneficial to consider why students all earned the top score. Perhaps the way this criterion was taught and practiced caused this perfect result. We certainly want to highlight any strategies that worked well so we continue to use them.

Half the students struggled with the Orient Reader criterion. This is an area where further instruction would be beneficial. The time to allot for the reteaching depends on whether students will encounter this type of writing again during the year. If they won't encounter it again, those students who struggled will benefit from additional lessons and practice prior to moving on. Perhaps having students rewrite the orientation section of their piece of writing will serve them well as a follow-up assessment. If students will be writing narratives throughout the year, the challenge area can be addressed as time goes on and may not be an immediate need.

Questions 7–10 in figure 6.4 provide some things to consider if reporting data for a group of students. Perhaps multiple students struggled with transitions. Small-group instruction and practice would be beneficial to eliminate the deficiency.

Notice that there is no confusion about what to reteach because the data directly connect to specific criteria. This will be the case anytime teachers report data based on the components of a standards-based rubric or an unpacked standard. Having a one-to-one correspondence between a data report and an unpacked standard will always provide guidance as to next steps. This will be the case with every example in this chapter; it will be true of all that you do as well. The concepts that you need to address again will be clear. What you do to address the concepts is flexible.

Teachers will have to decide what strategies to use to reteach. Discussing this topic with a team will result in multiple ideas to support student learning. Using a different strategy than what you originally used will be beneficial, as the first didn't result in the desired level of success. When your team collaboratively acts on common assessment results, perhaps the teacher who had the greatest success will work with the students who need the most support. Determine student strengths in each classroom, and share the strategies used to teach those concepts. Keep in mind that each classroom comprises students with different strengths and needs. Assessment results can vary due to the makeup of the classroom and not always the actions of the teacher. The students with the biggest challenges might mostly be in a single classroom. These students might be experiencing great growth, but teacher teams may not recognize it when comparing common assessment results. Take this into consideration.

The next example is based on a grade 1 Speaking and Listening standard. It asks students to orally describe people, places, things, and events. Students must also express their ideas and feelings about their descriptions. Figure 6.5 shares the unpacked standard.

Content Area: English Language Arts (Speaking and Listening)

Specific Standard: SL.1.4—Describe people, places, things, and events with relevant details, expressing ideas and feelings clearly.

Overarching Learning Target: My descriptions clearly express ideas and feelings.

Verbs or Actions	Receivers of the Actions	Additional Information (What, where, why, how, examples, teacher notes)	Detailed Learning Targets
Describe	People, Places, Things, and Events	With relevant details	I use details to describe people. I use details to describe places. I use details to describe things. I use details to describe events.
Express	Ideas and Feelings		When I describe people, places, things, and events, I use my ideas. When I describe people, places, things, and events, I use my feelings.

Source for standard: NGA & CCSSO, 2010a.

FIGURE 6.5: Unpacked document for Speaking and Listening standard 4, grade 1.

This standard asks students to create several different descriptions while also sharing ideas and feelings. It is likely that teachers will assess each description separately because of the students' age. Assessing all at one time could be overwhelming to the students. The assessment itself can be a simply stated assignment. Figure 6.6 provides an example.

Student directions as stated by the teacher:
Today, I am interested in hearing you describe a person so that I can listen to your skills as a speaker. You can describe a friend, a parent, a teacher, or someone else of your choice.
As you think about your description, remember to use details that will tell me more about the person. To help me understand the person, be sure to include ideas that relate to the person. Also, include how you feel about the person.
When I listen to the recording of your description, I will be comparing what you say to the rubric that we have been using when we've talked about this standard. You have a copy of the rubric so that you can refer to it as you are thinking about what to say.

FIGURE 6.6: Example assessment for Speaking and Listening standard 4, grade 1.

To evaluate student performance on a standard for speaking and listening, it is beneficial to have a consistent way of scoring. A rubric provides that consistency, ensuring that teachers score students using the same criteria and same common expectations. Figure 6.7 contains a rubric based on the unpacked standard in figure 6.5.

	1	2	3	4
Describe People	The description is unclear.	The description is clear.	The description is clear and detailed.	The description is clear and includes only relevant details.
Describe Places	The description is unclear.	The description is clear.	The description is clear and detailed.	The description is clear and includes only relevant details.
Describe Things	The description is unclear.	The description is clear.	The description is clear and detailed.	The description is clear and includes only relevant details.
Describe Events	The description is unclear.	The description is clear.	The description is clear and detailed.	The description is clear and includes only relevant details.
Express Ideas	Ideas are confusing or nonexistent.	Ideas are expressed and can be understood with careful concentration.	Ideas are expressed clearly.	Ideas are expressed clearly and relate to what is being described.
Express Feelings	Feelings are confusing or nonexistent.	Feelings are expressed and can be understood with careful concentration.	Feelings are expressed clearly.	Feelings are expressed clearly and relate to what is being described.

FIGURE 6.7: Example rubric for Speaking and Listening standard 4, grade 1.

Notice that the first four rows of descriptors are the same because they each evaluate a description, just based on a different subject. When evaluating the assessment in figure 6.6, we will use only rows 1 (Describe People), 5 (Express Ideas), and 6 (Express Feelings), since those rows directly relate to the contents of the assessment.

Because the rubric in figure 6.7 is being used to score the standard, the data template will be similar to figure 6.3 (page 113) with a few exceptions. The template in figure 6.8 reflects only the three rows of the rubric that teachers will use to score the assessment. In addition, in an attempt to show how color can help when analyzing data, 1s are shaded in a dark gray and 2s in a lighter gray. Students in need of support become easily apparent using this method. The Mode column on the right side of the data is divided into four so that each rubric score has its own column. This option makes it easier to see the number of students who earned each mode score. The students' mode scores are shaded in. If there is no mode, the median is shaded in, giving teachers another point of reference to consider.

	Describe People	Express Ideas	Express Feelings	Mode (or median when no mode)			
				1	2	3	4
Student 1	4	2	3				
Student 2	3	2	3				
Student 3	3	2	3				

FIGURE 6.8: Example data display for Speaking and Listening standard 4, grade 1.

continued ▶

	Describe People	Express Ideas	Express Feelings	Mode (or median when no mode)			
				1	2	3	4
Student 4	3	2	4				
Student 5	3	2	3				
Student 6	4	2	3				
Student 7	3	1	3				
Student 8	3	1	3				
Student 9	4	2	3				
Student 10	2	2	1				
Student 11	3	3	3				
Student 12	3	3	3				
Student 13	3	2	3				
Student 14	4	3	3				
Student 15	2	1	1				
Student 16	3	2	3				
Student 17	3	2	3				
Student 18	3	1	3				
Student 19	2	2	2				
Student 20	3	1	3				
	1s = 0 2s = 3 **3s = 13** 4s = 4	1s = 5 **2s = 12** 3s = 3 4s = 0	1s = 2 2s = 1 **3s = 16** 4s = 1				

Review the data in figure 6.8; then consider the following pieces of information. When looking across each row, you can see how each student performed. Students 10, 15, and 19 had difficulty with all aspects of their descriptions and need some additional practice and support. When looking down each column, you can see how the entire class performed. In this case, all but three students struggled with expressing ideas, and even those students have room for improvement. It appears as though students were pretty confident about expressing their feelings, but they struggled with ideas. Identifying what student needs are or how you can address them involves no guesswork. You look back at the way students were taught to express ideas and see what you can share to enhance student performance in this very specific area. You can mention examples and share descriptions followed by additional practice.

I'm confident that you have dozens of ideas about how you can reteach concepts that need to be addressed, but allow me to share a few here. If I were to go about reinforcing students' understanding of the challenge areas on this assessment, I'd first make sure my students clearly understand the difference between feelings and ideas; any confusion would need to be cleared up. We would engage in activities where students share ideas that they would suggest to people they know. We would go back and forth between sharing feelings and sharing ideas to distinguish between the two. We could choose a person who the class is familiar with and have multiple students share a single sentence describing the person, some students adding feelings and some adding ideas. This activity would continue until the class felt the person was well described according to our rubric. At that point, I would ask students to listen to the description they recorded and make changes and additions that they feel would enhance their work. These are just ideas, but they are easy to generate because the standard is clear on what students are to know and do and the assessment directly relates to the standard. There is no guesswork. The alignment is obvious.

MATHEMATICS EXAMPLES: NON-RUBRIC SCORED

Mathematics examples are next. Although they might look slightly different due to the subject, the process is the same, and the way data are organized is also the same. We'll start with a third-grade geometry example in which a standard asks students to understand the attributes of various quadrilaterals. In order to gather data, we will create an assessment that matches the criteria of the standard. We won't use a rubric for this assessment because, as with most mathematics assessments, the answers are either correct or incorrect and levels of quality are inapplicable. We will match the assessment items to the components of the unpacked standard and report data accordingly.

Figure 6.9 illustrates the unpacked standard. The standard asks that students understand the attributes of a rhombus, rectangle, and square. The word *understand* in the standard is important. The standard is not asking that students know or memorize the attributes; rather, it is asking that students understand the attributes and how they cause the shapes to fit into the category of quadrilaterals. When creating the assessment, focus on finding ways to have students demonstrate that they understand the components of the standard.

Content Area: Mathematics (Geometry)

Specific Standard: 3.G.A.1—Understand that shapes in different categories (e.g., rhombuses, rectangles, and others) may share attributes (e.g., having four sides), and that the shared attributes can define a larger category (e.g., quadrilaterals). Recognize rhombuses, rectangles, and squares as examples of quadrilaterals, and draw examples of quadrilaterals that do not belong to any of these subcategories.

Overarching Learning Target: I understand the attributes of four-sided shapes and how they can fit into the category of quadrilaterals.

Verbs or Actions	Receivers of the Actions	Additional Information (What, where, why, how, examples, teacher notes)	Detailed Learning Targets
Understand	Shapes	Share attributes	I understand that shapes share attributes, characteristics that are the same.
Understand	Shared attributes	Can define a larger category	I understand that shapes with shared attributes can fit into larger categories.
Recognize	Rhombus, Rectangle, and Square	Are quadrilaterals	I recognize that the attributes of a rhombus, rectangle, and square cause them to be quadrilaterals.
Draw	Quadrilaterals	That are not a rhombus, rectangle, or square	I draw shapes that are quadrilaterals but are not a rhombus, rectangle, or square.

Source for standard: NGA & CCSSO, 2010b.

FIGURE 6.9: Unpacked document for Geometry standard 1, grade 3.

The assessment in figure 6.10 has students demonstrate their knowledge of each component of the unpacked standard. Questions 1–4 are intended to ensure students recognize and understand the attributes of a rhombus, rectangle, and square. The standard states that the students need to understand all three. Question 5 asks students to choose every quadrilateral within a group of shapes, which demonstrates that students understand the characteristics of a quadrilateral. The task also reinforces the fact that the shapes can fit into the larger category. Question 6 asks students to draw two quadrilaterals that are not a rhombus, rectangle, or square, which is a requirement of the standard. Each question corresponds to a component of the standard, which will lead to data that are informative and actionable. The standard also invites the teacher to introduce students to other quadrilaterals if desired. The answer key for figure 6.10 can be found in figure 6.11.

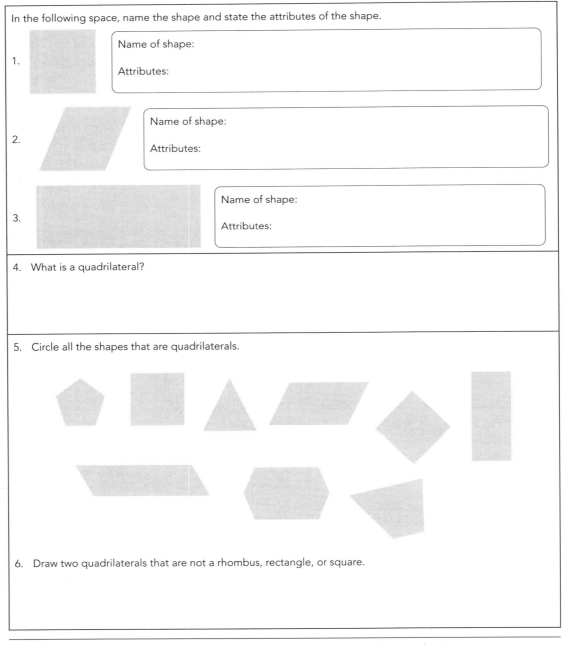

FIGURE 6.10: Example assessment for Geometry standard 1, grade 3.

In the following space, name the shape and state the attributes of the shape.

1.

Name of shape: Square

Attributes: 4 equal sides, 4 equal angles equal 2.

2.

Name of shape: Rhombus

Attributes: 4 equal sides, opposite angles equal 3.

3.

Name of shape: Rectangle

Attributes: 4 equal angles, opposite sides equal in length

4. What is a quadrilateral? A 4-sided figure

5. Circle all the shapes that are quadrilaterals.

6. Draw two quadrilaterals that are not a rhombus, rectangle, or square. Answers will vary.

FIGURE 6.11: Answer key for the example assessment based on Geometry standard 1, grade 3.

Organizing data in a consistent fashion allows for quick analysis because teachers do not need to decipher a new format. This assessment will use the unpacked standards document as the basis for its data format. Figure 6.12 shares an example of student data based on the assessment. Notice that the first and second categories are divided into three columns because there are three questions for each on the assessment. The first part of questions 1, 2, and 3 corresponds with Understand Shapes, and the second corresponds with Understand Shared Attributes. Recognize Quadrilaterals is divided into two columns because two questions deal with that component. Question 6 is the only one that assesses Draw Irregular Quadrilaterals, so that category has a single column. Shaded areas indicate incorrect responses.

	Understand Shapes			Understand Shared Attributes			Recognize Quadrilaterals		Draw Irregular Quadrilaterals
	1	2	3	1	2	3	4	5	6
Student 1									
Student 2									
Student 3									
Student 4									
Student 5									
Student 6									
Student 7									
Student 8									
Student 9									
Student 10									
Number of errors	0	4	0	0	4	0	1	1	2

FIGURE 6.12: Example assessment data display for Geometry standard 1, grade 3.

Let's review the information in figure 6.12. When comparing the errors displayed on the data chart to the assessment, we find that four students had difficulty naming and sharing the attributes of a rhombus. Two of those students were unable to draw a quadrilateral that is not a rhombus, rectangle, or square. Student number 3 also had difficulty recognizing quadrilaterals. After a quick analysis, we have a good amount of information. Next steps are easily identifiable. Four students need a small-group refresher about the attributes of a rhombus. Two of the same students also need to see some examples of irregular four-sided shapes. Student 3 understands the attributes of a square and a rectangle but is struggling with the concept of a quadrilateral. Because this student is working with other students to better understand the previously mentioned portions of the standard, a deeper understanding of quadrilaterals will be gained during the reteaching process. We can administer a brief assessment after reteaching. The assessment should concentrate on only those retaught components. This is to ensure that each student has made progress with these components. Students already demonstrated understanding of other portions of the assessment.

Next, we will look at a fifth-grade mathematics standard that deals with solving real-world problems using both fractions and mixed numbers. We will start with the unpacked standard, review an example assessment, and then share example data in a format similar to what we have been using. See figure 6.13 for the unpacked standard.

Content Area: Mathematics (Number and Operations—Fractions)			
Specific Standard: 5.NF.B.6—Solve real-world problems involving multiplication of fractions and mixed numbers, e.g., by using visual fraction models or equations to represent the problem. Overarching Learning Target: I solve real-world problems involving multiplication of fractions and mixed numbers.			
Verbs or Actions	Receivers of the Actions	Additional Information (What, where, why, how, examples, teacher notes)	Detailed Learning Targets
Solve	Real-world problems	Involving multiplication of fractions and multiplication of mixed numbers	I accurately multiply fractions in real-world problems. I accurately multiply mixed numbers in real-world problems.

Source for standard: NGA & CCSSO, 2010b.

FIGURE 6.13: Unpacked document for Number and Operations—Fractions standard 6, grade 5.

The assessment in figure 6.14 (page 124) lists five questions, all dealing with the multiplication of fractions and mixed numbers in real-world scenarios. In an effort to ensure students know the process, the assessment asks that students list the equation, show their work, and clearly identify their answer. Having them do all three will make it clear whether students understand and will be able to repeat the process. An answer alone doesn't provide the information we need to be confident students truly know the steps to achieve the appropriate outcome. The goal is not just to find an answer but to understand the process.

Read each real-world problem. Remember to do the following.
1. List the equation.
2. Show all work.
3. Clearly identify your answer.

1. Manny poured ½ of a cup of milk but drank only ⅓ of it. What fraction of a cup of milk did he drink?
2. Gina had ¾ of a candy bar. She gave the two of us ½ of it. How much of the original candy bar did each of us get to eat?
3. Darius was making cookies. Although the recipe asked for 1 ¾ cups of chocolate chips, he had only ½ that much. How many cups of chocolate chips did Darius have?
4. Mr. Wilton's fifth-grade class of 33 students is going on a field trip on Friday. The day after Mr. Wilton sent home permission slips, ⅓ of them were returned. How many students still need to return their permission slips?
5. Jordan has 12 video games. Marissa has 2 ½ times as many video games as Jordan. Jonas has ⅓ as many games as Marissa. How many games do Marissa and Jonas have?

FIGURE 6.14: Example assessment for Number and Operations—Fractions standard 6, grade 5.

Before you administer the assessment, it is helpful to clearly define expectations for students, which is the purpose of listing the three items in the directions. If further explanation is needed, share it prior to the assessment. For example, if you want the answer stated in a sentence, let students know that. Provide an example. Clearly identifying the answer for question 1 could mean students would state, "Manny drank ⅙ of a cup of milk," or you may allow "⅙ of a cup." It's up to you. Students will appreciate the clarity.

Figure 6.15 shows an example data display for the assessment in figure 6.14. The shaded areas indicate where errors occurred. In this case, some students struggled with identifying the answer in questions 4 and 5.

With each completed data display, we want to look at the results, celebrate areas of strength, and review errors. When we look at the assessment, we find that the students needed to complete a multistep problem. The first answer is not the final answer. Reviewing the student papers will tell us if next steps include reteaching multiplication of fractions or if students need a refresher on solving real-world problems. Once we determine which is the case, reteaching can be planned and implemented. In this case, reteaching may just include talking through the problems with the students so they can recognize and understand their mistake. If the errors are instead with multiplication and students are confused, we can implement a more formal reteaching plan. If many errors appeared on any assessment, and a great number of students were struggling, perhaps students would have benefited from additional instruction and practice prior to the assessment.

Whether the standard is in the area of English language arts or mathematics, the process used is the same.

1. Unpack the standard.

2. Create a rubric or an assessment that directly incorporates the components of the unpacked standard.

3. Administer the assessment, and place the results in a data format based on the unpacked standard.

4. Analyze the results, and determine next steps based on the components of the standard.

	Question 1			Question 2			Question 3			Question 4			Question 5		
	List equation	Show work	Identify answer	List equation	Show work	Identify answer	List equation	Show work	Identify answer	List equation	Show work	Identify answer	List equation	Show work	Identify answer
Student 1															
Student 2															
Student 3															
Student 4															
Student 5															
Number wrong	0	0	0	0	0	0	0	0	0	0	0	3	0	0	3

FIGURE 6.15: Example assessment data display for Number and Operations—Fractions standard 6, grade 5.

These four steps are powerful and provide a systematic path to student learning and achievement that benefits both teachers and students. Using a standards-based approach assists teachers in deeply understanding student expectations within the standards. As a result, they pass that knowledge on to the students. They design assessments that directly relate to the standards. They review data that align with expectations within the standards. Collaboration during the entire process encourages teachers to share ideas and learn strategies from each other that have proven successful with their students.

HOW TO DESIGN A SCOPE AND SEQUENCE

An experience I had when I went to a new district taught me the importance of a scope and sequence. I had none. As a result, being somewhat inexperienced at the time, I used the curriculum textbook as my scope and sequence. It had more than enough lessons for the entire year; in fact, it likely would have taken me a year and a half to get through the entire text, so I never really got to the later chapters. There is nothing wrong with using the text as a resource, but by not starting with the standards, I had no idea whether the text was always a match for what students really needed to do and know at that grade level. This school allowed grade levels to choose their own text, which was empowering, but that meant there wasn't necessarily alignment from text to text, level to level. I was uncomfortable. Was I teaching more than I needed to? Were there gaps that would cause my students to miss key concepts they would need for the following year? Did I need to get through the entire textbook? What could I skip? What was essential? With no standards-based scope and sequence, I just didn't know the answers. Truthfully, I think I did my best, and I'm confident that my students learned a lot, but I really didn't know if it was all they needed. I did my best with the tools I had.

The standards-based *scope and sequence* is a document that illustrates what teachers will teach in their instruction—the curriculum—and the time line for when they will cover it. The document takes the guesswork out of what to teach, enabling the purchase of resources that match identified needs within the scope and sequence of the curriculum. There is alignment across grade levels based on the alignment within the standards. This is clearly illustrated in figure 5.6 (page 94), which features Common Core Writing standard 1, grades 3–5.

The process to create a standards-based curriculum is identical to the process we have used throughout this book. We start with the unpacked standards; this time, we will unpack an entire domain. This step can be accomplished at any time. If you prefer to complete an entire domain as you are unpacking the standards, that works. Prior to this, we were learning the pieces; now, we are looking at the whole. This format gives us the ability to identify when we will teach the components of the standard.

Figure 6.16 provides an example scope and sequence for grade 1 Speaking and Listening standards. We would keep all the scope-and-sequence documents for the English language arts standards together to provide a comprehensive view of what is to be taught and in what time frame. Dates for common assessments can also be added to the documents if desired. Notice that all unpacked standards are listed on the same document.

Comprehension and Collaboration

SL.1.1: Participate in collaborative conversations with diverse partners about grade 1 topics and texts with peers and adults in small and larger groups.
   a. Follow agreed-upon rules for discussions (e.g., listening to others with care, speaking one at a time about the topics and texts under discussion).
   b. Build on others' talk in conversations by responding to the comments of others through multiple exchanges.
   c. Ask questions to clear up any confusion about the topics and texts under discussion.

Verbs or Actions	Receivers of the Actions	Additional Information	Au	S	O	N	D	Ja	F	M	Ap	Ma	Jn	Jl
Participate	In discussions	With diverse partners About grade 1 topics With peers With adults In small groups In larger groups		W1 W2										
Follow	Rules	For discussions		W1 W2										
Build	On conversation			W1 W2										
Respond	To others			W1 W2										
Ask	Questions	To clear confusion		W1 W2										

SL.1.2: Ask and answer questions about key details in a text read aloud or information presented orally or through other media.

Ask	Questions	About key details	W2 W3											
Answer	Questions	About key details	W2 W3											

SL.1.3: Ask and answer questions about what a speaker says in order to gather additional information or clarify something that is not understood.

Ask	Questions	About what a speaker says To clarify			W1 W2									
Answer	Questions	About what a speaker says To clarify			W1 W2									
Describe	People, Places, Things, and Events	With relevant details					W2 W3							
Express	Ideas and Feelings						W2 W3							

FIGURE 6.16: Scope-and-sequence document for Speaking and Listening standards, grade 1.

continued ▶

Verbs or Actions	Receivers of the Actions	Additional Information	Au	S	O	N	D	Ja	F	M	Ap	Ma	Jn	Jl
Presentation of Knowledge and Ideas														
SL.1.4: Describe people, places, things, and events with relevant details, expressing ideas and feelings clearly.														
SL.1.5: Add drawings or other visual displays to descriptions when appropriate to clarify ideas, thoughts, and feelings.														
Add	Drawings or displays	To clarify ideas, to clarify thoughts, and to clarify feelings					W2 W3							
SL.1.6: Produce complete sentences when appropriate to task and situation.														
Produce	Complete sentences		W2											

Source for standard: NGA & CCSSO, 2010a.

The columns that follow the unpacked standards represent the months of the school year from August to July using the abbreviations *A, S, O, N, D,* and so on. Listed next to each component is the week or weeks of that month (*W1, W2, W3,* and *W4*) in which the teacher will introduce the component. If the component will also be taught or formally reviewed at another point of the year, we can also identify that within the chart.

Once the components are taught, students are expected to use the standard throughout the year. For example, when students have learned the rules of discussion, the teacher should expect them to use those rules consistently. This is true of all standards that students regularly demonstrate, regardless of the subject. Of course, reminders may be necessary.

Next, let's look at a mathematics example in figure 6.17. The display format is identical. The unpacked standards for fourth-grade geometry provide an in-depth look at all that they ask of students. This scope and sequence would appear alongside all other categories of mathematics standards, including strands like numbers and operations, algebraic thinking, and whatever else your standards include. The complete set of documents provides a look at the year in advance, illustrating when concepts will be taught.

Draw and identify lines and angles, and classify shapes by properties of their lines and angles.														
4.G.A.1: Draw points, lines, line segments, rays, angles (right, acute, obtuse), and perpendicular and parallel lines. Identify these in two-dimensional figures.														
Verbs or Actions	**Receivers of the Actions**	**Additional Information**	**Au**	**S**	**O**	**N**	**D**	**Ja**	**F**	**M**	**Ap**	**Ma**	**Jn**	**Jl**
Draw	Lines and Angles									W1				
Identify	Lines and Angles									W1				
Classify	Shapes	By properties of lines and by properties of angles								W2				

Verbs or Actions	Receivers of the Actions	Additional Information	Au	S	O	N	D	Ja	F	M	Ap	Ma	Jn	Jl
Draw	Points, Lines, Line segments, Rays, Right angles, Acute angles, Obtuse angles, Perpendicular lines, and Parallel lines									W2 W3				
Identify	All	In two-dimensional shapes								W3				
4.G.A.2: Classify two-dimensional figures based on the presence or absence of parallel or perpendicular lines, or the presence or absence of angles of a specified size. Recognize right triangles as a category, and identify right triangles.														
Classify	Two-dimensional figures	On the presence or absence of parallel or perpendicular lines On the presence or absence of angles								W3				
Recognize	Right triangles									W4				
Identify	Right triangles									W4				
4.G.A.3: Recognize a line of symmetry for a two-dimensional figure as a line across the figure such that the figure can be folded along the line into matching parts. Identify line-symmetric figures and draw lines of symmetry.														
Recognize	Lines of symmetry									W4				
Identify	Line-symmetric figures									W4				
Draw	Lines of symmetry									W4				

Source for standard: NGA & CCSSO, 2010b.

FIGURE 6.17: Scope-and-sequence document for Geometry standards, grade 4.

The scope-and-sequence format is also useful to select or identify teacher resources. Schools accomplish this by comparing new or existing resources to the completed unpacked documents and determining which components are taught in which resources. Take a look at figure 6.18 (page 130) as an example. The standards are unpacked within the document. The last three columns relate to resources being reviewed. This document's purpose is to compare the resource to the components of the unpacked standards to determine whether there are gaps or overlaps. We can then make decisions as to which resource or resources will best meet the needs of the classroom. The *Xs* in each Resource column identify which components a resource addresses. The lack of an X makes it obvious that a resource does not address a component that needs to be taught. During a curriculum adoption, this handy chart takes the guesswork out of choosing textbooks. By *curriculum adoption*, I mean the time when a school, district, or state or province chooses to review what is taught at each level so that it can ensure alignment, eliminate overlaps, and review available resources that match the retooled curriculum. It identifies resources and purchases them, often by grade-level groupings, at the same time. It typically does this on a cycle that spans years. The chart provides evidence on which to base important decisions.

Purposes (Writing)
It is expected that students will:
Write clear, focused personal writing for a range of purposes and audiences that demonstrates connections to personal experiences, ideas, and opinions.

Verbs or Actions	Receivers of the Actions	Additional Information	Resource 1	Resource 2	Resource 3
Write	Clear	Personal writing	X	X	X
Write	Focused	Personal writing	X	X	X
Write	For a range of purposes		X		
Write	For a range of audiences		X		
Demonstrate	Connections to experiences, Connections to ideas, and Connections to opinions				

Thinking (Writing)
It is expected that students will:
Use writing and representing to express personal responses and relevant opinions in response to experiences and texts.

Verbs or Actions	Receivers of the Actions	Additional Information	Resource 1	Resource 2	Resource 3
Use	Writing	To express personal responses	X	X	
Use	Representing	To express personal responses	X	X	
Use	Writing	To express relevant opinions	X		
Use	Representing	To express relevant opinions			

Features (Writing)
It is expected that students will:
Use the features and conventions of language to express meaning in their writing and representing.

Verbs or Actions	Receivers of the Actions	Additional Information	Resource 1	Resource 2	Resource 3
Use	Features of language	To express meaning in their writing	X	X	
Use	Conventions of language	To express meaning in their writing	X		X
Use	Features of language	To express meaning in their representing	X	X	
Use	Conventions of language	To express meaning in their representing	X		X

Source for standard: Government of British Columbia, 2020.

FIGURE 6.18: Scope-and-sequence document for personal writing performance standards, grade 4.

Selecting resources can be emotional for some. They may have a favorite company or author. In order to make a standards-based decision, we try to take the emotion out of it and use a factual process. We should base the selection on how well the resources match the standards. Using the chart in figure 6.18 assists in that effort. After resources are reviewed for content and the selection is narrowed to those that rise to the top, other considerations come into play. Factors like cost, materials for special populations, availability of different languages, supplementary resources, and computer support systems can be considered to see which resources surface as the best ones available for the school, district, or state or province involved in the curriculum adoption.

The standards-based scope and sequence gives direction on what to teach and when but offers flexibility by not providing exact dates. It is a guideline that supports a continuous progression of learning and that can help in choosing resources that reinforce what the standards ask for. It is intended to support the teaching of all standards, providing longer periods of time to teach those that require additional emphasis at that grade level.

IN SUMMARY

The goal anytime we assess students is to gain a clear understanding of what they know and are able to do. In order to accomplish this, we create clear alignment among the standards, the learning targets, the assessments, and the data collected from the assessment results. This provides a linked approach to all that is taught and assessed. Because of this, alignment data are actionable. When students demonstrate a weakness, teachers can plainly see what they need to do to address the gap because of the direct link to the standard.

Implementing a consistent data display based on the unpacked standard is beneficial. The display allows teachers to easily identify next steps during data analysis. To support quick interpretation of the data, use a common display across classrooms, grades, or schools. Link assessments to the unpacked standard so all expectations of the standard are apparent and assessed. When reteaching is necessary, the data display creates an obvious picture of which portions of the standard need to be revisited and which students need additional support.

The unpacked document is a multipurpose tool. When teachers are determining when to teach curricular items, they can again employ the document. The document also provides a road map for the year and can be implemented across all subject areas.

The unpacked standards create the foundation for a perfect informative tool when purchasing resources. Comparing the resources to the components listed on the unpacked document will help identify the best choices for resource materials. Used during an alignment process, the document makes decision making data based. The document supports decisions based on fact and need during this often-confusing sales process.

Using the unpacked standard as the basis for reporting student data and building a scope and sequence will support continuing connections to the standard and a complete standards-based implementation, which is the subject of the next chapter.

PART 3

NEXT STEPS: EMBEDDING THE PROCESS

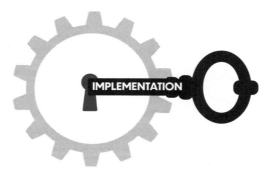

UNDERSTANDING STANDARDS

Implementing standards-based learning across grade levels, one school, or many schools requires embedding the process discussed throughout this book so that the impact is powerful, shared, and an automatic part of teaching and learning. Chapter 7 shares ideas and systems to embed the use of standards so that teachers can share the process with others and work together to experience success.

IMPLEMENTING THE PROCESS SCHOOL- OR DISTRICTWIDE

Why would we want to implement anything new in education? For me, the reasons are always associated with student success. How do we get students to learn and achieve at higher levels? How do we get them to understand what they are learning and why they are learning it? How do we better understand what we should teach and how our grade level impacts those beyond? I truly believe that a standards-based implementation is the answer. In my work with educators, I have seen their excitement while using the methods I discuss in this book. Excitement breeds excitement. Why would anyone get excited about what we are doing with standards? Because unpacking gives us new insights into the standards. But we don't stop there. Everything is connected. We then create standards-based learning targets that make sense to students and help them understand what they need to know and do to be successful. But we're not done. We now use the same templates and processes to create assessments and rubrics and collaboratively built common assessments. The pieces tie together. They make sense. They work. The effort we put into the process is rewarded with the outcomes that both staff and students enjoy. There is a strong feeling of accomplishment and, yes, even excitement!

When you want to extend standards-based processes beyond a single classroom, you might stumble. Sometimes, implementation fails. Clearly, that is not the desired outcome. But what can teachers and administrators do to support implementation? How can we increase our chances of success? How do we transition from professional learning to classroom implementation? Finding answers to these questions became of great interest to me. I taught and was an administrator in situations where implementations just faded away. I watched surrounding districts try other initiatives with limited success. The momentum just wasn't there. Frankly, we don't have time to waste, so failed implementations are frustrating. If we want an initiative to work, we need to plan, gain support, and move forward with a logical, sensible, meaningful plan and process.

As a result of my observations, I conducted a national survey on this topic as part of my dissertation. I asked teachers to respond to statements about the implementation of newly learned practices. More specifically, I asked them what would support their desire to implement a new practice. Teachers identified administrative expectation and support as the top reasons to implement; also highlighted was the importance of collaborating and working with peers as they learned and implemented new ideas, methods, and techniques (Depka, 2012). The results certainly seemed logical. Administrative support and expectation coupled with the ability to collaborate and implement with colleagues are a recipe for success. Research beyond my own reinforces the positive impact of administrative support and expectation as well as teacher collaboration. Shared instructional leadership and teacher collaboration result in improved student achievement (Goddard, Miller, Larson, & Goddard, 2010). Teachers and school leaders believe that their collaboration positively influences students' success, and it does (Burton, 2015; Jones-Goods, 2018). When teachers work together to discuss student achievement, they have a positive impact on student results (Mora-Ruano, Heine, & Gebhardt, 2019). When principals visibly demonstrate leadership as well as active involvement with teachers, they foster a learning community that is more likely to promote innovation and collaboration (Schleifer, Rinehart, & Yanisch, 2017).

I am confident that any teacher with the desire to do so can successfully implement standards. However, if the plan is to systemically embed practices, teachers should consider the power of mutual support and collaboration that go beyond a team or grade level. So how do we start?

Sharing practices with teachers across the school or district will serve to create a system that embeds standards-based instruction and positively impacts students. This chapter discusses a process for getting a school- or districtwide standards-based system off the ground. The process includes determining who will be involved, identifying and sharing the purpose, creating an implementation calendar, sharing and tracking progress, and celebrating.

DETERMINE WHO WILL BE INVOLVED IN IMPLEMENTATION

Implementation of standards-based learning might include several grade levels, a school, or a district. Even a small team of teachers or a grade-level team can start a process of implementation by learning the process and spreading the word. Depending on its size, the implementation initiative might be led by teachers, a team, administrators, or a mixed group of willing volunteers. Consider purchasing this book as a resource for each team member if funds are available. If not, having a few copies available will allow individuals to share and read it, giving the entire team firsthand knowledge of the process. It is also possible to have one or more individuals take the lead and teach the process highlighted throughout this book.

If you have already implemented the process that you have read about in this book, please consider sharing your progress with teaching partners to encourage their involvement. Working with a willing team will provide a supportive environment that includes a mutual goal and the sharing of ideas and work products. Your understanding and involvement will serve to pique the interest of your colleagues as you share the steps you have already taken. To provide guidance, examples, and a structured plan, use this book as the basis for continued next steps.

Perhaps the school leadership team determines that it wants to fully implement standards-based learning. Discuss who will most likely need to be involved so that the school experiences the highest levels of success. Will the leadership team teach the process? Are there others in the school who have experience that would be valuable to the implementation? What roles will the team members each play for the greatest chance at success?

Are you a principal who has decided that a standards-based implementation is the best course of action for your school? If so, who will help you lead the charge? When it comes to the implementation of standards, where are the pockets of promise in your school? Which teachers have already shared an interest or experienced success in the process? Determine who you want on the team, but also consider an open invitation for volunteers who want this leadership opportunity. Including a variety of representatives adds to the richness of the team. Consider classroom teachers, coaches, district personnel, individuals who have a fair amount of knowledge about the task, and others who have limited information but will perhaps provide fresh perspectives for the team.

When planning for a systemwide implementation as a district leader, start with or select your leadership team. School principals throughout the district need to be on board for the implementation to take hold. They are the school leaders and most often have in-depth knowledge of the personalities within the school and how best to achieve buy-in among teachers and other staff. Make everyone aware that, if the implementation is to be successful, principals need to take an active role and show that they expect and will actively support implementation. Teacher involvement will assist in promoting the learning and implementing of ideas within each school. Teachers also provide a mutual support system when learning and embedding new practices.

Whether you are an individual or group working toward implementation, this chapter is intended to guide you through a series of steps for integrating standards into everyday classroom, school, or district processes.

IDENTIFY AND SHARE THE PURPOSE

I can't think of a time in my life when I made a big change without having a reason for the change. I never moved just to move, for example. I moved when I had a need to be in a new location, or a growing family resulted in the need for a larger home. Likewise, when we are making a change in education, the reason should be clear. Educators shouldn't be left to wonder, *Why are we doing this?* The answers to this question should be addressed upon introducing the process used to implement standards. Taking the time to discuss the purpose will answer questions and help educators come to a clear understanding of why they should invest their time in this initiative. You could accomplish this through a book study or a review of articles dealing with standards. For a brief explanation, I suggest Apex Learning's (2017) blog post "Three Reasons Standards Are Essential to Educational Success." Mike Schmoker (2018), Robert J. Marzano (2017, 2018; Marzano, Norford, & Ruyle, 2019), and Thomas R. Guskey (2015, 2020) are authors who consistently show support for working with standards.

Perhaps your team already has enough expertise to have an informed discussion about why standards are important to education and student success. Communicate with those who would benefit from the message. This could be the team, school, or entire district, for example. The message might go like this:

We have heard about standards; our school [or district, state, province, or country] has standards. We have the need to work with them, but before we begin to discuss implementation practices, let's talk about this: Why should we put time and effort into systematically embedding standards in our classrooms? There are several reasons. Let's identify those important to us.

A few possible reasons for adopting standards-based learning include the following.

- Standards clearly state what students are to know and be able to do.

- Standards provide a way to measure student success.

- Standards help teachers plan what they need to teach students at each grade level.

- Standards give teachers information upon which to build assessments.

- Standards can help students understand what they are to learn.

- Standards provide consistency within and across classrooms.

- Standards highlight learning expectations.

- Standards give guidance as to the expected rigor of student performance on given standards. (Do students need to know? Recite? Explain? Analyze? Write?)

- Standards provide the foundation of learning discussions among teacher teams.

- Standards take the guesswork out of what to teach and to what extent to teach it at each grade level.

- Standards help with the selection of resources that will best meet student needs.

- Standards assist in evaluating program success.

- Standards help teachers identify rubric criteria.

- Standards provide the basis for feedback to students and parents.

- Standards can be used as part of a student-evaluation system.

- Standards identify criteria on which to base data collection in order to recognize student areas of strength and challenge.

After brainstorming a list of reasons why standards are important, consider creating a one- to two-sentence summary of the key reasons in your situation. Although this is not essential, it can serve as a good reminder for all stakeholders as implementation is underway. You can share the summary with both students and parents as your journey into standards continues so they remember the basis for your implementation. For example, the summary may mention that standards provide guidance to teachers and students about what students are to learn so they have a clear understanding of the progress needed to experience success. Instead of a single sentence, perhaps you would prefer to keep handy the entire list of reasons that you generated and ideas that the staff generated. The object is to clarify the reasons behind the use of standards so that people see the work of implementation as important and purposeful. This is meant to indicate not that current practices are wrong but that embedding standards can serve to support and enhance the status quo.

Also, identify the scope of the work. For example, the scope could be, "The fifth-grade team will be using *The Authentic Standards-Based Environment* to implement standards at the grade level." Or it could be, "The school district will use *The Authentic Standards-Based Environment* as a resource to implement standards at all elementary schools, and lead teams of teachers will introduce all aspects of the approach."

CREATE AN IMPLEMENTATION CALENDAR

An implementation calendar provides a progress goal and a commitment to completing the tasks that the implementation will require. It serves as a reminder of what needs to be accomplished and by when, and it gives direction for next steps. The calendar can also include information such as who is responsible for what implementation tasks. The calendar should be realistic. As with any implementation, team members need to have time allotted to meet and complete the work. The calendar must identify and build in time to make progress possible. Who has control of the calendar for the team? This may be an administrator or team member who has the ability to schedule times that will be available for all members. Seek permissions if they are needed. Consider, for example, the amount of time teachers need to read the corresponding chapter of this book, use the information within the chapter to create documents based on the standards they will implement, and use the information with students. Too little time can cause frustration. Too much time can result in stagnation. Figure 7.1 features an example implementation calendar and task list. (See page 146 for a reproducible version of this figure.) It is intended to be simple but meaningful.

Task	Due Date (Add the agreed-on date, time, and location.)	Discussion Leader (Add the team member's name.)	What to Do for the Meeting
Read chapter 1; use the template to unpack standards of your choice.			Bring the unpacked standards document to the meeting.
Read chapter 2; use the template to unpack another set of standards. Add learning targets.			Bring the unpacked standards document with learning targets to the meeting.
Read chapter 3; create an assessment based on a set of standards you have unpacked.			Bring the unpacked standards document and the assessment to the meeting.
Read chapter 4; create a standards-based rubric on the unpacked standard of your choice.			Bring the unpacked standard and rubric to the meeting.

FIGURE 7.1: Standards-based implementation calendar, version 1.

continued ▶

Task	Due Date (Add the agreed-on date, time, and location.)	Discussion Leader (Add the team member's name.)	What to Do for the Meeting
Read chapter 5; work with your team to create a standards-based assessment.			Bring the unpacked standards and ideas regarding the assessment design to the meeting.
Review chapter 5; collaboratively discuss the implementation procedures for the common assessment.			Identify the implementation procedures for the common assessment.
Read chapter 6; determine how common assessment data will be collected and displayed. Implement the common assessment.			Bring your thoughts about the common assessment implementation practices and the data discussion afterward so you can share them in the team meeting.
Collect and organize data from the common assessment. Be prepared to share and discuss the data at the team meeting.			Bring common assessment data in the designated format to the meeting. Discuss the data starting with the agreed-on questions. Determine and be prepared to implement next steps.
Implement the identified responses to data.			Share the successes and challenges of the responses to data. Review ideas to consider following the next common assessment.

With each new unit of study or set of standards, complete the following tasks.
1. Unpack standards.
2. Create learning targets.
3. Create standards-based assessments for the unit of study.
4. Create rubrics for the unpacked standards as needed.
5. Continue to record and display data for easy interpretation.
6. Continue to collaborate on the design, implementation, data review, and actions based on common assessments.
Continue to share throughout the process. Divide the tasks and share the products.

The good news is that most steps are, relatively speaking, not too time consuming. Once each step of the process is learned and used, it becomes a pattern used over and over throughout the year until all standards are addressed by the year's end. The calendar provides a step-by-step plan of what each component of standards-based implementation from the previous six chapters encompasses. Each step assumes rich discussion and sharing among colleagues. The number of meetings depends on the time available for each. More can be accomplished in a full day than in two hours, so schedule accordingly. The full team should be expected to attend each meeting so that information and input are available to all and the content of each meeting flows smoothly to the next. Accountability is important in that participants each have an obligation to complete their part of the plan by the identified due date.

Base due dates on the time available to teachers. A two-week time frame for each task is probably ideal in most situations. The team can extend this window if it so chooses, but this length of time allows all educators involved to remember what happened at the last meeting and continue the flow toward the implementation of standards. Lengthy gaps in progress can cause the process to slow and the team to waste time trying to remember and review previous progress.

When teams understand the process through reflection at the end of each planning cycle and through repetition of that cycle, they will increase their effectiveness with each new class of students, with any introduction of new standards, and with changes to team structures and membership. Teachers will reliably unpack standards and use them for all aspects of student learning again and again, each time with increasing proficiency. When teams of teachers are working with the same standards, it is also possible to divide and conquer. Members determine who will work with specified standards, complete the work, and share the outcome after each step highlighted in the calendar. All involved present their work to help others gain understanding, share ideas, and accept results. All educators are engaged in the task each step of the way.

Full effectiveness with the divide-and-conquer approach is achieved only after all involved are completely comfortable with the process. Stick together as a group and continue to share work products on the same standards until the confidence level is high. Working with partners from the team is also valuable. After confidence builds, the team can decide if it would like to work on different standards in order to make faster headway. Whatever the team chooses to do, a successful outcome can result. Work within the time frame that meets your needs and helps the work progress at a useful pace.

Notice that figure 7.1 describes the task; highlights what to bring to the meeting; shares a date, time, and location; and identifies a lead team member for each meeting. Creating a complete calendar in advance will promote the team's ability to stay on task within an identified time line. Adjustments are still possible if necessary. Think of the implementation calendar as similar to a scope and sequence. The goal is to stay on target in order to reach the desired outcome, but adjustments may need to be made along the way to arrive at the best result.

SHARE AND TRACK PROGRESS

We educators benefit from establishing a level of comfort with people we are expected to work closely with. If your implementation situation has teams working together whose members don't know each other, take time to have them get acquainted. Encourage team members to talk a bit about themselves, perhaps by responding to guiding questions or prompts like the following.

- Name one reason you chose to enter the field of education.
- Share one experience you have had in education that you will never forget.
- Why did you want to be part of this team?

Team members will get to know each other as they work together, but sharing at least some information initially will help them gain insights about one another. This will increase their comfort level, making discussions and work sessions more productive. It will also increase the willingness of individuals to share. Teams that consistently work together may already have established this level of comfort.

What expectations will be set for participants prior to the meeting? Reading the chapter in advance is a must in order to be acquainted with the process. If all teachers are working on the same set of standards, will they unpack the standards in advance and then share, discuss, and combine them at the meeting? Or will they unpack the standards collaboratively at the meeting? Either works. However, if teachers each unpack before the meeting, they will have increased familiarity with the process. This decision will need to be made ahead of each meeting by determining whether work in advance will benefit the team's progress. When all chapters have been read and everyone has engaged in each task for the first time, the team can choose whether it will assign members different standards to complete. In this way, the unpacking of standards and creation of learning targets could be completed for all standards at a faster pace. After completion, the entire team can review the work to gain understanding and agreement.

During each meeting, participants will be sharing their work products. Consider in advance how they will accomplish this. If all teachers are working on the same standards, they might choose to unpack the standards together for the first time to create consistency in practice and an increased comfort level. If desired, use a divide-and-conquer approach in which standards are divided among the group, unpacked individually, and shared back out with the group to establish ownership and understanding. Using a projection device, having a recorder available, and using a shared digital document, such as a Google Doc (https://docs.google.com), work well when discussing standards. No matter the method, the standards to unpack should be placed in the template in advance so the team can spend meeting time completing the task. If participants have unpacked different standards, the same methods will be effective. All the following meetings can use the same formats. The discussion leader for the meeting can be responsible for ensuring that everything to be shared is available and ready when the meeting begins.

Teams can easily track progress on the implementation calendar. Figure 7.2 provides another example of an implementation calendar; this one has a column to track progress and include additional implementation suggestions. (See page 148 for a blank reproducible version of this figure.) Both these examples are good options to use; the choice is just a matter of team preference.

What to Do Before the Meeting	What to Do at the Meeting	Date, Time, and Location	Organizer	Progress Made
Read chapter 1; choose some standards and unpack them to understand the process.	Using the process described in chapter 1, unpack the grade-level standards for reading informational text.	9/15 1:00 early release day Mr. S.'s room	Mr. S.	We completed unpacking all informational standards. We will continue with literature standards.

Read chapter 2; create learning targets for the previously unpacked standards to understand the process.	Using the process described in chapter 2, create learning targets for the standards for reading informational text.	9/29 1:00 early release day Miss T.'s room	Miss T.	We created all learning targets for informational standards. We will continue with literature standards.
Read chapter 3; use the recommendations to create an assessment for standards currently being taught.	Create a common assessment for the unpacked reading standards.	10/14 Full professional development day Office conference room	Mrs. L.	We created assessment tasks. Mrs. L. volunteered to place the assessment in a student-ready format.
Read chapter 4; unpack your choice of writing standards. Create a sample rubric to share with the team at the next meeting.	Share the rubrics that team members created. Use the documents to create a team rubric.	11/13 3:00 Office conference room	Mrs. Z.	We designed a team rubric combining suggested wordings from team members' individual rubrics.
Read chapter 5; review the procedures for implementing a common assessment.	Discuss common assessment implementation procedures. Determine the team responses.	11/27 3:00 Miss R.'s room	Miss R.	Miss R. recorded all the team's agreed-on procedures in a Google Doc.
Read chapter 6; consider the ideas presented. Be ready to discuss them at the team meeting.	Identify how data from the common assessment will be represented. Discuss initial questions to be used during the data discussion.	12/12 1:00 early release day Office conference room	Mr. M.	Mr. M. recorded the data procedures in a Google Doc. A template for data was also created.
Collect and organize data from the common assessment.	Share, discuss, and compare data, and determine next steps.	1/25 1:00 early release day Office conference room	Mr. M.	Data were shared and discussed. Everyone will implement their next steps.
Implement agreed-on next steps following the common assessment data discussion.	Create a time line for continuing the process of embedding standards throughout the school year.	2/11 Full professional development day Office conference room	Mrs. Z.	We all recorded next steps in a Google Doc. The plan is to have all English language arts standards unpacked with learning targets by the end of the school year with one common assessment created for each standard category.

FIGURE 7.2: Standards-based implementation calendar, version 2.

Structure the implementation calendar in a way that best meets your needs and keeps you on track to achieve implementation goals. Realistically, there may be delays. Sometimes, they are unavoidable. Major district or school projects, illness, state or province testing windows, or unexpected schedule interruptions could cause them. Be open about the causes of delays. Determine what needs to be done to get back on track, and move forward. The calendar dates should be adjusted to show the updated time frame. A commitment to the updated calendar is important so that you keep to the schedule as closely as possible. This will help build and maintain momentum for the implementation. Be careful to recognize and eliminate excuses that delay progress. Excuses can stem from a lack of commitment to implementation and can be caused by the concern of even one individual. Address concerns, re-establish the focus, and secure the commitment. Concerns can result from a lack of understanding of the process. At each meeting, you may start with a brief review of each chapter's key points followed by an opportunity for team members to ask questions. Do not take concerns personally. They are what they are. Work together to solve issues with an eye consistently on the target. Be open to giving and accepting feedback. Collectively, the strengths and knowledge of the team will provide the insights that will lead to success.

CELEBRATE: SHARE TESTIMONIALS AND SUCCESSES

It's easy to forget to pause and say, "This is going well." When we are doing a good job, we should celebrate successes at each step. Celebration can energize teams. It will support motivation and commitment to the process. Even if there are bumps along the way, we can overcome them, and when we do, we should celebrate! Celebrating the small successes leads to the accomplishment of larger goals. When team members feel positive about their team and their work, they will accomplish higher levels of achievement (Amabile & Kramer, 2011).

Consider having a sharing time at the onset of each meeting. Limit the time frame so it doesn't consume the whole meeting, but share new ideas. Ask for one or two sentences from each participant so that everyone has a chance to share while keeping on schedule. Encourage participants to articulate their successes and spread the word about techniques and implementations that went well. I often hear teachers share comments from students that they like the use of the unpacked standards and learning targets because it gives them increased clarity about what they are expected to learn and how they are expected to perform.

Of course, with sharing comes the ability to use each other's best ideas as implementation continues. Success breeds success. Motivation will continue, and the desire to increase the scope of the work will be the result.

IN SUMMARY

When the desire is to implement standards-based learning beyond a single classroom, determine who will be involved in the implementation. Perhaps a grade-level or learning team will be part of the group. If a school- or districtwide implementation is the plan, choose individuals who will spread the word and commit to a successful outcome. Remember to have an avenue for volunteers to join your efforts. The goal is to be inclusive and encourage participation from those who have the interest or passion to do so. Participants should have a good idea of their role before committing to the work.

Clearly communicate the purpose of the work. In fact, communicate to all who will be impacted by the work. Why is a standards-based implementation valuable to both educators and students? How will the implementation support current work? How will the implementation positively impact everyone? Know why the work is to be started, and be clear to others as to what the intention is and why it will positively impact those involved.

The Authentic Standards-Based Environment provides a step-by-step approach that will support the work of implementation. Create an implementation calendar to provide a time frame in which the initial work is expected to be completed. This should include expectations for the participants as well as meeting times to share or carry out the work. The calendar is intended to keep the project moving at an appropriate pace.

Share and track progress in order to recognize what has been accomplished and be clear on next steps. Collaboration plays an essential role in the implementation. An atmosphere of trust and support promotes progress. Tracking the work creates a diary of progress toward the goal and identifies what comes next. It helps the process advance smoothly.

Finally, celebrate the work as it progresses. Consider and share the impact on students. Share ways the implementation is impacting the classroom. Identify stories that highlight student success as a result of standards-based learning. Remember that this work will help students succeed, and nothing is more important.

Standards-Based Implementation Calendar, Version 1

Task	Due Date (Add the agreed-on date, time, and location.)	Discussion Leader (Add the team member's name.)	What to Do for the Meeting
Read chapter 1; use the template to unpack standards of your choice.			Bring the unpacked standards document to the meeting.
Read chapter 2; use the template to unpack another set of standards. Add learning targets.			Bring the unpacked standards document with learning targets to the meeting.
Read chapter 3; create an assessment based on a set of standards you have unpacked.			Bring the unpacked standards document and the assessment to the meeting.
Read chapter 4; create a standards-based rubric on the unpacked standard of your choice.			Bring the unpacked standard and rubric to the meeting.
Read chapter 5; work with your team to create a standards-based assessment.			Bring the unpacked standards and ideas regarding the assessment design to the meeting.
Review chapter 5; collaboratively discuss the implementation procedures for the common assessment.			Identify the implementation procedures for the common assessment.
Read chapter 6; determine how common assessment data will be collected and displayed. Implement the common assessment.			Bring your thoughts about the common assessment implementation practices and the data discussion afterward so you can share them in the team meeting.
Collect and organize data from the common assessment. Be prepared to share and discuss the data at the team meeting.			Bring common assessment data in the designated format to the meeting. Discuss the data starting with the agreed-on questions. Determine and be prepared to implement next steps.

page 1 of 2

Task	Due Date (Add the agreed-on date, time, and location.)	Discussion Leader (Add the team member's name.)	What to Do for the Meeting
Implement the identified responses to data.			Share the successes and challenges of the responses to data. Review ideas to consider following the next common assessment.
With each new unit of study or set of standards, complete the following tasks. 1. Unpack standards. 2. Create learning targets. 3. Create standards-based assessments for the unit of study. 4. Create rubrics for the unpacked standards as needed. 5. Continue to record and display data for easy interpretation. 6. Continue to collaborate on the design, implementation, data review, and actions based on common assessments.			Continue to share throughout the process. Divide the tasks and share the products.

Standards-Based Implementation Calendar, Version 2

What to Do Before the Meeting	What to Do at the Meeting	Date, Time, and Location	Organizer	Progress Made
Read chapter 1; choose some standards and unpack them to understand the process.	Using the process described in chapter 1, unpack the grade-level standards for reading informational text.			
Read chapter 2; create learning targets for the previously unpacked standards to understand the process.	Using the process described in chapter 2, create learning targets for the standards for reading informational text.			
Read chapter 3; use the recommendations to create an assessment for standards currently being taught.	Create a common assessment for the unpacked reading standards.			
Read chapter 4; unpack your choice of writing standards. Create a sample rubric to share with the team at the next meeting.	Share the rubrics that team members created. Use the documents to create a team rubric.			

page 1 of 2

What to Do Before the Meeting	What to Do at the Meeting	Date, Time, and Location	Organizer	Progress Made
Read chapter 5; review the procedures for implementing a common assessment.	Discuss common assessment implementation procedures. Determine the team responses.			
Read chapter 6; consider the ideas presented. Be ready to discuss them at the team meeting.	Identify how data from the common assessment will be represented. Discuss initial questions to be used during the data discussion.			
Collect and organize data from the common assessment.	Share, discuss, and compare data, and determine next steps.			
Implement agreed-on next steps following the common assessment data discussion.	Create a time line for continuing the process of embedding standards throughout the school year.			

REFERENCES AND RESOURCES

Ainsworth, L. (2015, February 24). *Priority standards: The power of focus*. Accessed at www.edweek.org /education/opinion-priority-standards-the-power-of-focus/2015/02 on February 8, 2022.

Amabile, T. M., & Kramer, S. J. (2011, May). The power of small wins. *Harvard Business Review*. Accessed at https://hbr.org/2011/05/the-power-of-small-wins on April 5, 2022.

Anderson, L. W., & Krathwohl, D. R. (Eds.). (2001). *A taxonomy for learning, teaching, and assessing: A revision of Bloom's taxonomy of educational objectives* (Complete ed.). New York: Longman.

Apex Learning. (2017, January 16). *Three reasons standards are essential to educational success* [Blog post]. Accessed at www.apexlearning.com/blog/3-reasons-standards-are-essential-to-educational-success on May 4, 2022.

Bloom, B. S. (Ed.). (1954). *Taxonomy of educational objectives: Book 1—Cognitive domain*. New York: Longman.

Burton, T. (2015). *Exploring the impact of teacher collaboration on teacher learning and development*. Doctoral dissertation, University of South Carolina. Accessed at https://scholarcommons.Sc.edu/etd/3107 on May 5, 2022.

Center for Teaching Innovation. (n.d.). *Using rubrics*. Accessed at https://teaching.cornell.edu/teaching -resources/assessment-evaluation/using-rubrics on January 21, 2022.

Center on Standards and Assessment Implementation. (2018). *Standards alignment to curriculum and assessment*. Accessed at https://files.eric.ed.gov/fulltext/ED588503.pdf on January 18, 2022.

Chowdhury, F. (2019). Application of rubrics in the classroom: A vital tool for improvement in assessment, feedback and learning. *International Education Studies, 12*(1), 61–68. Accessed at https://eric.ed .gov/?id=EJ1201525#:~:text=A%20rubric%20is%20a%20useful,their%20own%20quality%20of%20 work on January 21, 2022.

Depka, E. (2012). *From professional development to implementation: What teachers say makes change happen*. Unpublished doctoral dissertation, Cardinal Stritch University.

Depka, E. (2017). *Raising the rigor: Effective questioning strategies and techniques for the classroom*. Bloomington, IN: Solution Tree Press.

Depka, E. (2019). *Letting data lead: How to design, analyze, and respond to classroom assessment.* Bloomington, IN: Solution Tree Press.

Eaker, R., & Marzano, R. J. (2020). *Professional Learning Communities at Work and High Reliability Schools: Cultures of continuous learning.* Bloomington, IN: Solution Tree Press.

Erkens, C. (2015). *Collaborative common assessments: Teamwork. Instruction. Results.* Bloomington, IN: Solution Tree Press.

Farnsworth, S. (2017, June 3). *Help me unpack the standards: A framework for teacher and student clarity* [Blog post]. Accessed at https://shaelynnfarnsworth.com/2017/06/03/help-me-unpack-the-standards-a-framework-for-teacher-student-clarity on March 29, 2022.

Fisher, D., Frey, N., Amador, O., & Assof, J. (2018). *The teacher clarity playbook, grades K–12: A hands-on guide to creating learning intentions and success criteria for organized, effective instruction.* Thousand Oaks, CA: Corwin Press.

Francis, E. M. (2022). *Deconstructing Depth of Knowledge: A method and model for deeper teaching and learning.* Bloomington, IN: Solution Tree Press.

Gershon, M. (2018). *How to use Bloom's taxonomy in the classroom: The complete guide.* Blairsville, PA: Learning Sciences International.

Goddard, Y. L., Miller, R., Larson, R., & Goddard, R. (2010, May 3). *Connecting principal leadership, teacher collaboration, and student achievement* [Paper presentation]. Presented at the annual meeting of the American Educational Research Association, Denver, CO. Accessed at https://files.eric.ed.gov/fulltext/ED528704.pdf on April 4, 2022.

Government of British Columbia. (2020). *British Columbia performance standards.* Accessed at www2.gov.bc.ca/gov/content/education-training/k-12/teach/resources-for-teachers/curriculum/bc-performance-standards on January 18, 2022.

Guskey, T. R. (2015). *On your mark: Challenging the conventions of grading and reporting.* Bloomington, IN: Solution Tree Press.

Guskey, T. R. (2016, October 14). *Standards-based learning: Why do educators make it so complex?* Accessed at www.edweek.org/education/opinion-standards-based-learning-why-do-educators-make-it-so-complex/2016/10#:~:text=An%20emphasis%20on%20%E2%80%9Cessential%20questions,students%20achieve%20those%20learning%20goals on January 21, 2022.

Guskey, T. R. (2020). *Get set, go! Creating successful grading and reporting systems.* Bloomington, IN: Solution Tree Press.

Hattie, J. (2012). *Visible learning for teachers: Maximizing impact on learning.* New York: Routledge.

Herk, M. (2015, November 23). *6 takeaways from scores on the new Common Core–aligned tests* [Blog post]. Accessed at www.ced.org/blog/entry/6-takeaways-from-scores-on-the-new-common-core-aligned-tests on January 21, 2022.

Jones-Goods, K. M. (2018). A phenomenological study of teacher collaboration using a professional learning community model. *Journal of Research Initiatives, 3*(3), Article 10. Accessed at https://digitalcommons.uncfsu.edu/cgi/viewcontent.cgi?article=1155&context=jri on May 5, 2022.

Kansas State Department of Education. (2011, May 3). *A cautionary note about unpacking, unwrapping, and/or deconstructing the Kansas Common Core standards.* Accessed at www.k-state.edu/ksde/alp/resources/CautionaryNote-Module5.pdf on April 15, 2022.

Kaufman, J. H., Opfer, V. D., Bongard, M., Pane, J. D., & Thompson, L. E. (2018). *What teachers know and do in the Common Core era: Findings from the 2015–2017 American Teacher Panel* [Research brief]. Santa Monica, CA: RAND. Accessed at www.rand.org/pubs/research_briefs/RB10035.html on January 21, 2022.

Kornhaber, M. L., Barkauskas, N. J., & Griffith, K. M. (2016). Smart money? Philanthropic and federal funding for the Common Core. *Education Policy Analysis Archives, 24*(93), 1–37.

Lipton, L., & Wellman, B. (2012). *Got data? Now what? Creating and leading cultures of inquiry.* Bloomington, IN: Solution Tree Press.

Maimaran, M. (2017). To increase engagement, offer less: The effect of assortment size on children's engagement. *Judgment and Decision Making, 12*(3), 198–207.

Marzano, R. J. (2017). *The new art and science of teaching.* Bloomington, IN: Solution Tree Press.

Marzano, R. J. (2018). *Making classroom assessments reliable and valid.* Bloomington, IN: Solution Tree Press.

Marzano, R. J., Norford, J. S., & Ruyle, M. (2019). *The new art and science of classroom assessment.* Bloomington, IN: Solution Tree Press.

McCluskey, N. (2010). *Behind the curtain: Assessing the case for national curriculum standards* (Policy Analysis No. 661). Washington, DC: Cato Institute. Accessed at https://files.eric.ed.gov/fulltext /ED520384.pdf on January 21, 2022.

Michigan Virtual Learning Research Institute. (2020, September 1). *How implementing voice and choice can improve student engagement* [Blog post]. Accessed at https://michiganvirtual.org/blog/how-implementing -voice-choice-can-improve-student-engagement/ on March 31, 2022.

Mora-Ruano, J. G., Heine, J.-H., & Gebhardt, M. (2019). Does teacher collaboration improve student achievement? Analysis of the German PISA 2012 sample. *Frontiers in Education, 4.* Accessed at www.frontiersin.org/articles/10.3389/feduc.2019.00085/full on May 5, 2022.

Moss, C. M., & Brookhart, S. M. (2012). *Learning targets: Helping students aim for understanding in today's lesson.* Alexandria, VA: Association for Supervision and Curriculum Development.

National Governors Association Center for Best Practices & Council of Chief State School Officers. (2010a). *Common Core State Standards for English language arts and literacy in history/social studies, science, and technical subjects.* Washington, DC: Authors. Accessed at www.corestandards.org/assets/CCSSI _ELA%20Standards.pdf on February 14, 2022.

National Governors Association Center for Best Practices & Council of Chief State School Officers. (2010b). *Common Core State Standards for mathematics.* Washington, DC: Authors. Accessed at www.corestandards.org/assets/CCSSI_Math%20Standards.pdf on February 14, 2022.

Nichols, H. (2022). *Finding your blind spots: Eight guiding principles for overcoming implicit bias in teaching.* Bloomington, IN: Solution Tree Press.

Nielsen, M. (2016, July 19). *Unpacking standards leads to confidence, not chaos, for teachers and students.* Accessed at https://allthingsassessment.info/2016/07/19/unpacking-standards-leads-to-confidence-not -chaos-for-teachers-and-students on January 21, 2022.

Ragupathi, K., & Lee, A. (2020). Beyond fairness and consistency in grading: The role of rubrics in higher education. In C. S. Sanger & N. W. Gleason (Eds.), *Diversity and inclusion in global higher education: Lessons from across Asia* (pp. 73–95). Singapore: Palgrave Macmillan.

Scherer, M. (2001). How and why standards can improve student achievement: A conversation with Robert J. Marzano. *Educational Leadership, 59*(1), 14–18.

Schimmer, T. (2016a). *Grading from the inside out: Bringing accuracy to student assessment through a standards-based mindset.* Bloomington, IN: Solution Tree Press.

Schimmer, T. (2016b, May 26). *Repacking standards.* Accessed at https://allthingsassessment .info/2016/05/26/repacking-standards on March 29, 2022.

Schleifer, D., Rinehart, C., & Yanisch, T. (2017). *Teacher collaboration in perspective: A guide to research.* Brooklyn, NY: Public Agenda. Accessed at www.in-perspective.org/files/PublicAgenda _TeacherCollaborationInPerspective_AGuideToResearch_2017.pdf on April 2, 2022.

Schmoker, M. (2018). *Focus: Elevating the essentials to radically improve student learning* (2nd ed.). Alexandria, VA: Association for Supervision and Curriculum Development.

Schmoker, M., & Marzano, R. J. (1999). Realizing the promise of standards-based education. *Educational Leadership*, *56*(6), 17–21.

Stiggins, R. (2005). From formative assessment to assessment for learning: A path to success in standards-based schools. *Phi Delta Kappan*, *87*(4), 324–328.

Stiggins, R. (2014). Improve assessment literacy outside of schools too. *Phi Delta Kappan*, *96*(2), 67–72.

Texas Education Agency. (2017). *Texas Essential Knowledge and Skills*. Accessed at https://tea.texas.gov /academics/curriculum-standards/teks/texas-essential-knowledge-and-skills on April 19, 2022.

Timperley, H. (2009, August 17). *Using assessment data for improving teaching practice* [Paper presentation]. Presented at the 2009 Australian Council for Educational Research conference. Accessed at https://research.acer.edu.au/cgi/viewcontent.cgi?article=1036&context=research_conference on January 21, 2022.

Webb, N. L. (2002). *Depth-of-knowledge levels for four content areas*. Accessed at https://apps.web.maine.gov /doe/sites/maine.gov.doe/files/inline-files/dok.pdf on September 16, 2021.

Wiggins, G., & McTighe, J. (2012). *The Understanding by Design guide to advanced concepts in creating and reviewing units*. Alexandria, VA: Association for Supervision and Curriculum Development.

INDEX

S

T

Letting Data Lead
Eileen Depka

Rely on *Letting Data Lead* to help you build a culture of data analysis and student achievement in your school or classroom. This practical resource clearly outlines a systematic approach for conducting effective assessments, collecting meaningful data, and taking action based on the results.
BKF839

Raising the Rigor
Eileen Depka

This user-friendly resource shares questioning strategies and techniques proven to enhance students' critical thinking skills, deepen their engagement, and better prepare them for college and careers. The author also provides a range of templates, surveys, and checklists for planning instruction, deconstructing academic standards, and increasing classroom rigor.
BKF722

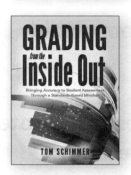

Grading From the Inside Out
Tom Schimmer

The time for grading reform is now. While the transition to standards-based practices may be challenging, it is essential for effective instruction and assessment. Discover the steps your team can take to transform grading and reporting schoolwide.
BKF646

Assessment as a Catalyst for Learning
Garnet Hillman and Mandy Stalets

Embrace a fresh mindset where the assessment process is a gift to students and propels meaningful learning for all. With this resource as your guide, you'll learn how to work individually or collaboratively to intentionally identify and unwrap priority standards, develop learning progressions, design assessments, and plan daily instruction.
BKG007

Unpacking the Competency-Based Classroom
Jonathan G. Vander Els and Brian M. Stack

Explore a variety of perspectives and examples from educators who have shifted to CBE with great results. The book details how to do the work by reevaluating and revamping traditional policies, structures, and procedures, including assessment and instruction practices.
BKG018

Solution Tree | Press

a division of
Solution Tree

Visit SolutionTree.com or call 800.733.6786 to order.

Wait! Your professional development journey doesn't have to end with the last pages of this book.

We realize improving student learning doesn't happen overnight. And your school or district shouldn't be left to puzzle out all the details of this process alone.

No matter where you are on the journey, we're committed to helping you get to the next stage.

Take advantage of everything from **custom workshops** to **keynote presentations** and **interactive web and video conferencing**. We can even help you develop an action plan tailored to fit your specific needs.

Let's get the conversation started.

Call 888.763.9045 today.

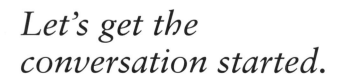

 SolutionTree.com